GREAT
LAKES
COOKERY

*Heritage Stories and
Recipes for the Four
Seasons*

by Bea Smith

✌ GREAT LAKES COOKERY ✌

Heritage Stories and Recipes for the Four Seasons
by Bea Smith

Published by Avery Color Studios, Inc.
511 D Avenue
Gwinn, MI 49841

Printed and manufactured
in the United States of America

Copyright 1991
by Avery Color Studios
ISBN #0-932212-82-4
Library of Congress #91-70624

First Edition March 1991
Reprinted 1992
Reprinted 1995
Reprinted 1998

Table of Contents

❧
GREAT LAKES
COOKERY
❧

℘

PREFACE

℘

A lifetime is too short to experience the full beauty of our northern seasons. I often wonder about what my mother and her mother saw through their kitchen windows as they prepared meals for their families. Many of the foods that they cooked and served are still old-time favorites. So, I like to cook those old-fashioned meals experiencing a feeling of security in our fast changing world, while knowing that the best of the past is still with us. In "Great Lakes Cookery – Heritage Stories and Recipes for the Four Seasons" I have tried to give you the new and easy methods to put together most of those delicious meals in our modern kitchens.

I wish to thank Marge Cotter from the Traverse City Record Eagle and Pat and Jim Silbar of the Charlevoix County Press who have been publishing my articles through the years. When I think of the many wonderful friendships that have resulted from them, I am overwhelmed with appreciation and thanksgiving.

Yes! I see beauty every season of the year from my kitchen window.

In appreciation,
Bea Smith
December, 1990

Spring

There is an elusive magic in the out-of-doors these early spring days in our North Country. The cold nights and sunny days start the sap running in the sugar maples, a crocus sprouts up as the snow melts in a sunny spot; so we feel spring in the air as we watch the first robin then the white-throated, white-crowned and fox sparrows on their trip further north. When pussy willows come out along the sides of the country roads we are ready to welcome spring. As the old saying goes, "spring has sprung."

Plowing time is a celebration of spring. We have faith that the planting will follow and the seeds will grow. Maybe that speck of faith was born within me because as a child I loved to walk behind him in the furrow that the plow made when Papa guided it in long straight rows across the field. With his hands on the handles of the plow and the lines to the horses tied around his middle, he plodded on. He would occasionally let go of the handles just long enough to guide the horses; they knew what to do.

Now, sometimes it grieves me a little that I am no longer close to the soil. We seldom see anyone plowing any more—the big machines cover many acres in a day. I like to think of people plowing all over the world. Hopefully wars will stop long enough for peaceful men to plow with faith in the future, to feed our hungry world.

ᔑ
GREAT LAKES
COOKERY
ᔑ

Maple Syrup Time

*I*f I were a poet, I would write an ode to the sugar maple—how it tells us goodbye in October with its bursts of indescribable colors of red, yellow and gold. Then when we think that spring will never come and we are bogged down with cabin fever, the sap begins to rise in the maples. The rise and fall of temperatures, from cold nights to warmer days, starts the sap flowing.

The Indians in our Great Lakes area were prepared for this, as they produced maple sugar and syrup long before the white man settled in America. In fact, maple sugar and maple syrup were the main sources of sweetening for the early Colonists, though they did have wild honey and molasses that was shipped from the West Indies.

Many old-timers have fond memories of going to sugaring-off parties, where spoonfuls of hot syrup were dropped in the snow to harden. My husband recalled the time his class from Benzonia Academy had a day off from school to visit a nearby sugar bush. Since I was a very young child, I have pondered on where the name "sugar bush" originated. I am still pondering. I remember thinking that it must have been a very large bush loaded down with maple sugar candies. I still wonder why a grove of beautiful maple trees is called a bush.

Every year the maple trees lining our village streets are tapped and buckets are filled with the "sweet water," as it was called by the Indians. A few years ago someone with an innovative sense of humor even tapped a telephone pole in the village of Boyne Falls. I wonder how many people drove around the block like we did just to see if what we saw was really there.

One does not really need any extra special recipes for maple syrup. Mother made baking powder biscuits and served sauce dishes of maple syrup to dunk the hot buttered biscuits. What a wonderful dessert for a later winter supper! Now is the time to make your special pancakes. I have given you a recipe for oatmeal pancakes before; however, this one is made light with buttermilk.

Hardscrabble Oatmeal Cakes

3/4 C. quick rolled oats
1-1/2 C. buttermilk*
1/2 t. soda
1 egg, beaten
1/2 C. sifted flour
1 T. sugar
3/4 t. salt
butter
*(I use the dry buttermilk mix for this)

Mix oats with buttermilk and let stand 10 minutes. Then add other ingredients, mixing well. Let stand to blend for a few minutes. If batter is too thick, add more buttermilk; if too thin, add a tiny bit of flour. Grease the griddle; fry pancakes in butter over low heat on both sides. This takes just a little longer to brown than regular pancakes. Of course, serve these pancakes with maple syrup!

*N*ext is a delicious casserole of sweet potatoes with maple syrup. Add some delicious fried pork sausage and you have another early spring supper.

Baked Sweet Potatoes and Apples

3 large apples   1 t. salt
3 T. butter   1/2 C. maple syrup
3 large sweet potatoes, boiled and skinned

Pare, core and slice apples; fry them in butter until light brown. Slice the potatoes. Arrange the apples and potatoes in layers in a buttered baking dish. Sprinkle with salt. Pour the syrup over the dish and dot with more butter. Bake 350 degrees about 35 minutes. Crumbled corn flakes may be put on the top of this dish before dotting with butter.

St. Patrick's Day

In my research I have discovered that St. Patrick's favorite herb was garlic. His cook always carried a good supply of garlic while he was traveling throughout Ireland. Maybe he knew something that took us centuries to rediscover. Garlic has healthful qualities. It now is considered to be an aid to a healthy heart as it contains a natural blood thinner.

What interesting things we discover when we probe into the past. I remember asking my father, "Why do we celebrate St. Patrick's Day?" He said that St. Patrick chased all of the snakes out of Ireland. I grew up with lots of questions about Ireland. I still have them and I am inspired by the Irish people and their wonderful philosophy about life with their famous sayings like "May you have a full table and gratitude in your heart."

Emerald Green Soup

*S*t. Patrick's Day is the time for the "Wearin' of the Green"—the color of the three-leaf shamrock. We need to serve something green also. In place of the traditional corned beef and cabbage, you can serve the brisket of beef with onions and carrots, if you wish, but use the cabbage in the following soup.

3 T. vegetable cooking oil
1 bunch scallions, chopped
1 clove garlic, minced
1 medium potato, peeled and chopped
3 to 3-1/2 C. chicken broth
1 lb. small cabbage, shredded
1/2 lb. spinach, stem removed, leaves
    chopped
1-1/2 C. skim milk
1 to 3 T. dry sherry
Chopped parsley for garnish

Heat oil in large pot; add scallions and garlic. Cook over medium heat until scallions are transparent; add potato and broth. Cover; bring to a boil. Add shredded cabbage and spinach. Cook, uncovered, until potato is soft and cabbage tender. Whirl half of mixture at a time in blender or food processor; return to pot. Add milk; bring to a boil. Stir in sherry. Serve garnished with chopped parsley.

My friend, Nony Irey of Pawcatuck, Connecticut, makes this soda bread and her family loves it.

For dessert, use your favorite recipe for cheesecake or do it the easy way with a boxed mix. Just before serving the chilled cheesecake, decorate it using the green of kiwi fruit.

Nony's Irish Soda Bread

3 C. flour	1-1/2 C. raisins
2/3 C. sugar	2 eggs, beaten
1 T. baking powder	1-3/4 C. buttermilk
1 t. baking soda	1 T. melted butter or
1/2 t. salt	margarine

Stir dry ingredients together in bowl; stir in raisins. Combine eggs, buttermilk and butter or margarine; add to dry ingredients, mixing just until flour is moistened. Add about 1/4 cup of buttermilk if needed, to mix well. Turn batter into a loaf pan or 2-quart casserole that has been sprayed with vegetable spray.

Cut a 1/4-inch deep, 4-inch-long slit in top of bread if using loaf pan. If using casserole, cut a 4-inch long, 1/4-inch deep cross in the top. Bake in preheated oven at 350 degrees for 1 hour, until bread bounces back when lightly touched. Remove from pan immediately; cool thoroughly before slicing.

Kiwi Fruit Topping

4 kiwi fruits, peeled and thinly sliced
2 T. orange marmalade, sieved

Arrange sliced fruit on cake; brush with sieved marmalade.

April Green

April is here and we are thinking of salads. I believe that it must be an inherited age-old longing for fresh vegetables when our land is suddenly turning to delicate shades of green. Even if we get one more coating of snow over April's touch of green, we know that it is temporary and an April snow is beneficial to crops.

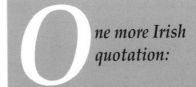

One more Irish quotation:

"May the hand of a friend be near you. May God fill your heart with gladness to cheer you."

The birds that I have fed survived the winter storms and everything is starting to grow again. We can dream of those fresh vegetables growing in our gardens. Though I no longer have a garden, I still glory in those beautiful seed catalogs.

It seems that anything goes in salads today. I believe that we have learned some of this at our restaurant salad bars. There are salads for every occasion. This first one is a meal in itself. I chose this at Sipples Restaurant in Clearwater, Florida, where we had a get-together of old friends. Cornbread and bran muffins were served with this salad, making this luncheon memorable. This salad could be used as a side salad for dinner if you use smaller amounts and serve on a salad plate.

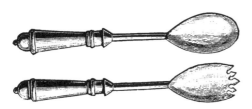

Garden Pasta Salad

Lettuce leaves
Head lettuce, chopped
3/4-inch chunks ham and chicken breasts
White cheese chunks
1/2 C. cooked pasta shells or corkscrews
Tomatoes, quartered

Divide ingredients among salad plates. Pour Italian dressing over all; garnish with tomatoes.

My friend and neighbor, Amy Courtney, brought in a serving of this salad for my dinner recently. I have made it a few times since because I received a small blender for Christmas that chops the carrots fine. Amy's salad dressing makes this salad so very special for me.

This next salad is a little more exotic dish. Serve it for a special luncheon or for a leisurely family meal. They will want to try it with different condiments.

Amy's Carrot and Raisin Salad

For each cup of grated carrots:
1 large or 2 small apples, peeled and diced, and/or
1 small can pineapple chunks, drained
1/4 C. raisins

Salad Dressing:
Mix 1/2 C. of canned coleslaw dressing with 2 T. of mayonnaise. Mix carrots, apples and/or pineapple and raisins together. Stir salad dressing into carrot salad; chill before serving.

Indian Style Apple Salad

1 qt. shredded head lettuce
3 Golden Delicious apples
1 pkg. (8 oz.) imitation crab or regular crab, canned or frozen
Curry Dressing (recipe follows)
Condiments: Salted peanuts, toasted sesame seeds, sunflower seeds, raisins, chutney, chopped hard-cooked egg.

Put lettuce into chilled bowl, cut apples in quarters, core and slice thinly. Arrange apples and crab over lettuce. Toss with curry dressing. Makes 6 servings.

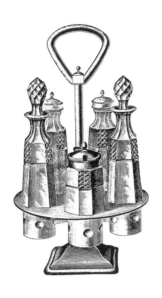

Curry Dressing

2/3 C. vegetable oil
1/2 C. white vinegar
1/2 t. curry powder
1/2 t. onion powder
1/2 t. white pepper
Dash of cayenne

Combine oil, vinegar, curry powder, onion powder, white pepper and cayenne; mix. Let stand 1 hour to blend flavors; makes 1-1/2 cups. Arrange dishes of condiments around salad and toss at table.

Eggs and Easter Memories

My early memories of Easter are definitely connected with eggs. During the long, cold winter months the hens stopped laying. Mother was making eggless cakes and scrimping on the egg sandwiches in our school lunch pails. Then the few warm days before Easter the hens started laying again, and we continued the tradition of eating as many eggs as we wanted.

Easter Brunch

Fruit Juices

Ellery's Turkey Sausage*

Rolls or Biscuits

Corn Cheese Pudding*

Swiss Layered Salad*

Raspberry Meringues*

*Recipe included

My husband told me about one Easter when he and his brother, two farm boys, were left on their own; their mother had taken a train trip to Berrien County to visit friends and relatives. Imagine them trying to eat as many fried eggs as they could hold, racing to see which one could eat the most. They never heard of cholesterol; both boys were probably considered "skinny" and both lived to a robust 80 years old. They also ate lots of butter on home made bread.

My friend, Ellery, tells about his early years as a fisherman's son in Connecticut. He remembers when a big bowl of hard-boiled eggs was the centerpiece for their Easter dinner; it was a real treat. When he was a young boy (he is now nearing 80), his mother bought their milk from a man who came daily and poured their milk into a pitcher from a large container. When she had milk to make rice pudding it was a special treat. The fishermen had gardens and sometimes raised a pig to be butchered in the fall. They traded fish for eggs and other farm produce. Ellery said that they had plenty of good food but little money.

So for old time's sake, let's not completely eliminate the egg in our diet; we need protein and it is a good supply for it. We can cut down on the cholesterol in other ways, like this Easter brunch featuring Ellery's turkey sausage.

Turkey Sausage

About 2 lbs. ground turkey
2 t. salt
2 t. poultry seasoning
1 t. pepper
2 t. sage
1 t. sugar

Mix all the ingredients and let sit in the refrigerator a day or two. Form into small patties and fry as for any hamburger or meatballs. The sugar helps it to brown. Ellery made this for me and I found it delicious.

Corn Cheese Pudding

4 eggs
1-1/2 C. milk
3 C. corn (canned and drained or fresh)
1/2 C. chopped onions
1/2 C. chopped peppers
1 t. salt
1/4 t. pepper
1 C. grated Cheddar cheese
1-1/2 C. soft bread crumbs

A casserole dish is always fine to serve for a brunch, and this next recipe from Jackie Rathbon is one of Ellery's favorites. This could be prepared the night before to have ready to bake in the morning.

Preheat oven to 350 degrees. Beat eggs; add milk, corn, onions, peppers, salt, pepper and cheese. Mix well and transfer to a baking dish. Top with crumbs. Cover and bake for 30 minutes. Take cover off and bake 15 minutes more or until brown. Serves 8.

Jackie Rathbon, Pawcatuck, Connecticut

For a brunch we like to have everything made ahead when possible. This next salad should be refrigerated for at least 12 hours, ready to serve at any time.

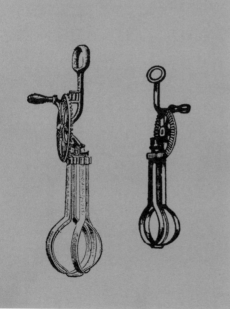

Swiss Layered Salad

In a long, flat 2-quart casserole place a layer of fresh chopped spinach; over this sprinkle salt and pepper and sugar. Over this crumble one pound of crisp cooked bacon. Add a layer of 6 hard-cooked eggs, sliced—save some for the top. Over this put a layer of chopped lettuce; sprinkle again with salt, pepper and sugar. Spread with 1 (10 oz.) package uncooked frozen peas. Add a layer of sliced large sweet onion. Over all spread 1 cup mayonnaise and 1 cup of Miracle Whip mixed together. Sprinkle with grated Swiss cheese and add a few slices of egg. Refrigerate 12 hours. Serves 12.

Raspberry Meringues

This meringue can be made up to five days ahead for your convenience, and will make six 4-inch meringue shells or about nine smaller ones. You might want to make two separate recipes for a large crowd. I do not recommend doubling this recipe.

3 egg whites at room temperature
1/4 t. cream of tartar
3/4 C. sugar
1/4 C. finely chopped hazelnuts or pecans
1/2 t. vanilla

Preheat oven to 275 degrees. In small bowl with the mixer at high speed, beat the egg whites and the cream of tartar until soft peaks form. Gradually sprinkle in the sugar, beating after each addition about 2 minutes, then beat until the sugar is completely dissolved. Test this by pinching a little bit between your thumb and finger to see if it is gritty. If so, keep on beating until it is smooth. Gently fold in the nutmeats and vanilla. (You may, instead, put the nuts on the pan you bake the meringues in—just a few under each meringue.) Onto a large greased cookie sheet, spoon mixture into six 4-inch mounds or nine 3-inch ones; with a spoon make into nest shapes. Bake 45 minutes until they are crisp and very lightly browned. Turn off oven; let meringues stand in oven 45 minutes longer to dry. Cool completely on cookie sheets. Store loosely wrapped in waxed paper and keep at room temperature.

Make the raspberry sauce and store in the refrigerator.

Raspberry Sauce

1 pt. pkg. frozen raspberries, thawed
About 1/4 C. sugar (a good time to taste for sweetness)

Cook until all sugar is dissolved. When ready to serve, fill each shell with a scoop of your very best vanilla ice cream and top with the raspberry sauce.

The Most Delicious Mushrooms

From the World Book Encyclopaedia:

"One of the most delicious of the mushrooms is the morel. The cups look like cone-shaped sponges pitted like a honeycomb. Grows best among leaves or wood ashes." Our town has its mushroom festival every year in early May, and mushroom lovers from all over Michigan and surrounding states will be here in Boyne City to hunt for those delicious morels and celebrate the National Mushroom Festival.

I like to go morel hunting, but I have to admit that my companions always find more than I do. I can walk right over them and never see one. I have been told that you should look ahead to see those shapes above the leaves. However, I always find them where I least expect to, very close to home, in the driveway or when I am out for a walk and not looking for them.

Morels are easy to identify, but be sure to see that the hollow top portion of the plant extends to the base of the plant. Any mushroom looking like a morel that is attached the same way an umbrella is fastened to the handle is not a morel. Throw those out!

We all love those delicious morels just fried in butter with a little salt and pepper. I think it is the favorite way to eat them. However, here are some recipes from a cookbook published in 1908. The housewives fixed mushrooms in various ways. They lived off the land more than we do and made good use of plants and herbs from the woods and fields.

Joe's Steak Sauce

1 T. margarine or butter
1 small onion chopped
1 can (4 oz.) of sliced mushrooms, drained
1/2 of a medium-sized bottle of A-1 Sauce

In a small skillet melt the butter and cook the onions until barely tender; add the mushrooms and A-1 Sauce and cook a few minutes more, then pour over steak.

Deviled Mushrooms

Mix 1 teaspoon dry mustard, a few grains of cayenne, 1 teaspoon Worcestershire sauce and 1/2 teaspoon paprika. Cover broiled mushrooms with mixture and serve on a slice of toast.

I'm sure that scalloped mushrooms were favorites because the old timers liked sauces on almost everything. I think this recipe will be very good with the tender flavor of morels.

Scalloped Mushrooms

Clean 1 lb. mushrooms and saute in butter. Arrange layers with white sauce in buttered baking dish; when filled, cover with cubes of bread that have been dipped in melted butter. Brown in the oven and serve.

Man has eaten mushrooms since a very early time. The Greeks and Romans were fond of them. More people in Europe than in America eat them regularly. Our ancestors most likely knew how to pick the non-poisonous kinds before they came to America. Here, they have long been considered a table delicacy rather than a main food, though they have been a staple food in the very southern part of South America and in some parts of Australia.

Writers of the old cookbooks took it for granted that everyone knew how to make white sauce. I do it this way:

White Sauce

For one cup of sauce, melt 1 tablespoon butter or margarine in a small skillet. Add 1 tablespoon flour and stir until smooth, then gradually add one cup of milk, stirring constantly, until thick and smooth. Season with salt and pepper. Double this for most recipes.

There are only 10 calories in a half cup of mushrooms, sliced or chopped raw; just think what they add to a salad. There are 21 calories in the canned kind with the liquid; what an addition to that steak sauce or for Beef Stroganoff.

Here is a modern recipe using canned mushrooms.

Broiled Mushrooms

If you have a few nice big ones, do it this way; clean them your regular way— most people soak them in salted water for a little while and drain dry, then broil 12 large ones and place on rounds of toast. Saute a cup of chopped mushrooms in 2 tablespoons butter, season with salt and pepper and add 1/4 cup heavy cream. Reheat and pour over mushrooms on toast.

Tuna Chow Mein

1/4 C. chopped onion
1/4 C. chopped green pepper
1/2 C. celery slices
2 T. butter
1 can (4 ozs.) sliced mushrooms
2 T. soy sauce
1 T. cornstarch
1 can (9-1/2 ozs.) tuna, drained, flaked
1 C. cottage cheese
3 C. cooked hot rice

Saute onion, green pepper and celery in butter until crisp-tender. Drain mushrooms, reserving liquid. Add enough water to liquid to make 1/2 cup; add soy sauce. Blend liquid into cornstarch. Add to vegetables; cook until thickened, stirring constantly. Add mushrooms, tuna and cottage cheese to vegetable mixture; mix lightly. Heat thoroughly. Serve over rice. Garnish with green pepper rings if desired.

Rhubarb—Spring's First Fruit

Rhubarb actually is a vegetable; however, we are not going to worry about that. How we used to long for Mother's first pie-plant pie. Rhubarb does have a cathartic effect and our grandmothers thought that it was good to clean out the system every spring. They, no doubt, were right.

The earliest historical record about rhubarb came from China about 2700 B.C. During those times, its roots were used for medicines. It came to Europe much later, reaching Italy about 1600. Maybe the reason for this was the fact that the leaves and roots of rhubarb are poisonous; only the stalks are edible. About 25 or 30 years later it was well known in England and used for pies and tarts. It became widespread in the colonies during the 1700s.

*T*angy sweet and tart rhubarb fills that need for fresh fruit when late April and May arrive and fruits and berries are not yet ripe.

I think another reason it did not become popular earlier in history is because it needs quite a lot of sweetening. I recall that during World War II we did not fix rhubarb because sugar was rationed and we used it sparingly.

Now, I am one who longs for that sweet and tart taste of early spring rhubarb or "pie plant" as some people call it. Rhubarb is a perennial and does not adapt to warm climates. It requires a winter's rest with a long cold period to thrive year after year. In Northern Michigan it grows to perfection. We've also discovered that rhubarb grows in Scotland. We were amazed to see the size of rhubarb plants growing on the grounds at Dunvagun Castle on the Isle of Skye. Leaves were over a foot in width. We were not surprised when rhubarb pudding with cream was served that night at Oig Hotel. It reminded me of Mother's rhubarb pudding.

I have made this pudding using biscuit mix with a little sugar and butter added to the batter, though I have had to settle for a dab of whipped topping for the cream.

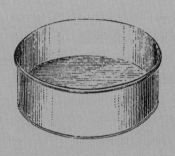

I have been saving this next recipe for the fresh rhubarb. I hope you like it—an extra plus to the old-fashioned pudding.

Mother's Rhubarb Pudding

She made this pudding with the first tender shoots of rhubarb before the plants provided enough for a pie. She made it in a pudding dish, or what she called a milkpan. Milk pans were used to hold the milk until the cream rose to the top, the cream spooned off to make butter—this was before the cream separator was invented. They were like large cake pans with sides 3-1/2 to 4 inches high. She lined the bottom of the pan with cut-up rhubarb sprinkled generously with sugar, then put spoonfuls of biscuit batter on top. She served this pudding with fresh cream. This was my father's favorite dessert for dinner at noon on the farm.

Rhubarb Crisp

Filling:

1-1/2 C. sugar	3 T. flour
1/4 t. salt	1 T. lemon juice
2 eggs, beaten	1 T. butter, melted
4 C. rhubarb, diced	

Combine sugar, flour, salt, lemon juice, eggs and butter; mix in rhubarb. Pour into 8 x 8 x 2-inch pan or 9-inch pie pan.

Topping:
3/4 C. sugar
1/2 C. flour
2 T. grated orange rind
1/3 C. softened butter

Mix until crumbly all ingredients listed. Sprinkle over filling. Bake at 375 degrees about 50 minutes until crisp and brown.

Rhubarb Crunch

1 C. flour	3/4 C. rolled oats
1 C. brown sugar	1/2 C. butter

6 C. small cubes of rhubarb, about 2 lbs.
1-1/2 C. sugar
1 C. orange juice or apple juice
3 T. cornstarch

In medium bowl combine flour, oats and brown sugar; cut in butter with pastry cutter or two knives until mixture resembles coarse gravel. Press 3/4 of the mixture into bottom of a 9 x 13 x 2-inch baking pan. Cover with evenly-cubed rhubarb and set aside.

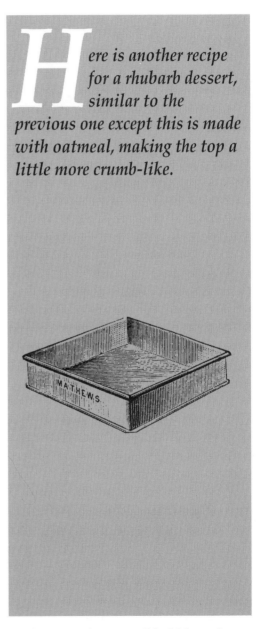

Here is another recipe for a rhubarb dessert, similar to the previous one except this is made with oatmeal, making the top a little more crumb-like.

In medium saucepan combine sugar, orange or apple juice and cornstarch. Bring to a boil over medium heat, stirring constantly, until sauce is thickened and clear. Pour evenly over rhubarb and sprinkle with flour mixture. Bake at 350 degrees about one hour, until bubbly and lightly browned on top. Makes 8 to 10 servings.

I wanted something different made with rhubarb, so I made this dessert adapting a couple of old-time recipes. This is easy to make and good to have handy when warm days arrive.

Rhubarb Mousse

1 C. cooked rhubarb
Sugar to taste (1/2 C.+)
1 C. whipping cream
1/2 t. almond extract

Cut the rhubarb in 1/4-inch slices and cook in just enough water to cover the bottom of the pan. It makes its own juice and needs to cook about 10 minutes. Cool. Sweeten to taste.

Whip the cream until stiff; add the cooled rhubarb. Sweeten with some powdered sugar if it needs it. Stir in almond extract.

The Bob-O-Link, The Rice Bird

Every spring I watch for that happy bird, the bright, yellow, white and black bob-o-link. I even drive out on county roads where I have seen them before, and low and behold, about the middle of May there he is singing to his mate.

In the 1879 edition of McGuffy's Reader, the poem "Robert of Lincoln" was used as a moral lesson "worthy of the attention of all little birds and boys" not to overindulge as the bob-o-link does when he is old and fills himself up on rice. In South Carolina he is called the rice bird because he plays havoc with the rice crop, gorging himself so he can hardly fly. However, I still enjoy reading John Logan's "Robert of Lincoln".

"Merrily swinging on brier and weed
Near to the nest of his little dame,
Over the mountainside or mead.
Robert of Lincoln is telling his name
Bob-O-Link, Bob-O-Link
Spink, Spank, Spink"

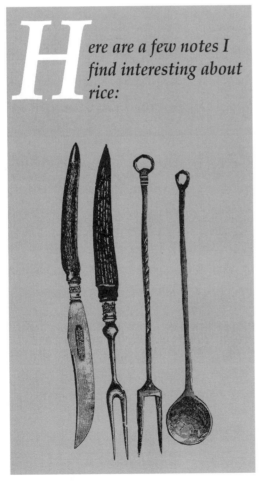

*H*ere are a few notes I find interesting about rice:

- Rice grew wild in prehistoric India and tropical Southeast Asia.

- About one-half of the world's population is almost wholly dependent upon rice.

- Many Asians eat rice three times a day and often very little else.

- It was first grown in America in South Carolina.

- The United States exports thousands of bushels every year, even to the South Pacific nations.

- The United States ranks among the leading exporters of rice, though it furnishes only a little over 1% of the world's crop.

*T*he places to find rice recipes are in the old cookbooks. Our grandmothers cooked rice in varied ways. It was a wholesome staple, inexpensive, a good "keeper" and easy to digest—especially the way they made rice pudding. On the farm Grandma had lots of good milk and a fire going in the cookstove, so it was no problem to put a dish of pudding into the oven for a couple of hours.

Indian Rice Pudding

(Lowneys Cookbook, Pub. 1908)

4 C. milk	1/4 C. rice
1/2 C. molasses	2 T. butter
1/2 t. ginger	1/4 t. salt

Mix ingredients in order given, pour into deep baking dish, set in a pan of hot water and bake two hours. Stir once during cooking. (For Indian Rice Pudding with apples, add 2 C. pared and quartered apples before baking.)

Rice Balls for Soup

1 C. cold cooked rice	2 T. flour
Salt, cayenne, nutmeg	1 egg
1 t. grated lemon rind	
1 t. chopped parsley	

As you can see, the old recipe did not specify what quantity of spices to use. In this case the cooked rice was most likely salted while cooking. Cayenne is very hot, so go easy here—less than 1/8 t. perhaps. Taste for nutmeg; some families like lots of nutmeg, others do not.

Mash rice or put through sieve. Add flour, egg and seasonings. Roll into balls, allowing a teaspoon for each ball. Cook in boiling salted water until they harden on the outside. Serve hot with soup.

Green Peppers

Cut off the tops of green peppers; remove the seeds and parboil peppers for about 5 minutes.

Cook 1 C. rice in chicken stock until tender. (I use chicken bouillon for this). Add 1/4 C. finely chopped onion, 2 T. red pepper or pimento finely chopped, 2 T. melted butter, a few chopped mushrooms (a small can drained is O.K.) Season with salt and pepper.

In filling the peppers you might need to add a little more chicken stock or hot water if the filling is real thick. This should fill 6 medium-sized peppers. Bake in pan in a moderate oven until lightly browned and piping hot.

You might want to save some cooked rice for the next time you serve most any kind of soup, especially beef or vegetable.

Homegrown, fresh green peppers soon will be available at our garden markets, and here is a delicious way to use them.

A Role-Model Mom?

While browsing through a modern magazine recently, I read that when women hear people telling them that they are just like their mothers, many liked the idea; however, some women resented this. I think it is only natural for most women when very young to think that they know more than their mothers, but this is something most of us outgrow. As a mother in her 70s I can look back to my mother and grandmother with love and understanding. When I look into my mirror now, I see that I look more like my mother every day and I like the idea. I am happy to have had a role model in my mother.

Our mothers might not always be wise in their decisions for us or themselves; however, they are forever wise in their love. I also can look ahead for my daughters and granddaughters and know that they will experience this wonderful love that seems to be eternal, as far as mothers are concerned. They are and will be role models to the future generations.

*M*aybe this Mother's Day we mothers can concentrate on being role models and accept the gifts and honors with a deep appreciation, whether we deserve it or not.

Now, what can we prepare for Mother to express this special kind of love? Children can learn at an early age to be a part of this celebration. The very young can help to make this fun salad from an old cookbook.

Bird's Nest Salad

Rub a few drops of green food coloring into cream cheese; mix well, using a little at a time for delicate color, like bird's eggs. Roll into balls the size of bird's eggs; arrange some small well crimped lettuce leaves on a flat dish, grouping to look like nests. Moisten with French dressing; place 5 balls in each nest of leaves. The cheese balls can be varied by flecking with black, white or red pepper.

At the "Chefs' Taste" gathering at Shanty Creek, the chef from Garland served Lingonberry Sauce on Smoked Venison. It was delicious and reminded me that it is time to visit Punzel's Swedish Gift Shop near Buckley. I love to go there and I always buy my favorite lingonberry preserves.

Lingonberry Torte

4 oz. unsweetened chocolate
1 C. milk
1 C. flour   1/2 t. salt
2-1/2 t. baking powder
4 eggs plus 1 egg yolk   1-1/2 C. sugar
2 t. almond extract

Lingonberry jam *or substitute currant or whole cherry preserves*

Butter Cream Frosting *(following)*

Combine chocolate and milk in top of double boiler; cook over hot water until chocolate melts, stirring frequently. Or melt the chocolate in a glass dish in the microwave. Cool. Sift flour, salt and baking powder together; set aside. Beat eggs and extra yolk with rotary or electric mixer until light and thick; add sugar gradually, beating until mixture is very smooth. Stir in almond extract and chocolate milk mixture. Sift flour mixture on top, folding gently but thoroughly; pour into 2 9-inch greased cake pans. Bake in preheated 350 oven for 10 minutes. Reduce heat to 325; continue baking 25 to 30 minutes until toothpick inserted in the center comes out dry. Cool several minutes; invert on cake rack to cool completely.

Spread lingonberry jam or preserves between layers; frost top with this butter cream frosting.

You could make this delicious lingonberry torte for Mother, even if she is not Swedish. She will be delighted.

Butter Cream Frosting

1/2 C. softened butter	2 T. milk
1-1/2 C. confectioners' sugar	1/2 t. vanilla

Combine all ingredients; beat with electric beater until smooth and thick, adding extra sugar if necessary.

I realize that this recipe is rich in calories, sugar and those other goodies, but Mother's Day only comes once a year.

This next recipe, typically, is not a stir fry but it makes a delicious breakfast, lunch, or supper-in-a-skillet. It has that down-home old time flavor which we long for occasionally.

Stir Cooking May Date to Cave Days

Stir cooking is not new although it has a new name. Stir-fry cookery, no doubt, goes back to the time when a cave man or woman mixed some meat and vegetables on hot stones. By the time that iron pots and skillets—or spiders as they were called—were invented, almost everything was fried. Grandma's "warmed-up potatoes" mixed with onions and/or any other vegetables she had left over was stir-fried for supper. Flannel hash made with left over cubed corned beef, onions, chopped potatoes and cooked beets was a popular dish in Colonial times. It still is a good classic recipe.

The way that we stir-fry is new, however; we do not overcook our vegies like Grandmother did.

We use a variety of non-cholesterol oils to fry the colorful vegetables and fruits, our meat, and we even add some cheese in the last few minutes for a complete meal—so nourishing, so tasty and beautiful to behold.

Country Sausage and Fried Apple Rings

Core unpeeled apples of any tart variety, slice into 1/2-inch rings. Shape sausages into patties; fry in heavy skillet until well done but not crisp. Transfer to heated platter; keep warm. Leave sausage fat in skillet; add as many apple rings as will fit in. Sprinkle with brown sugar and cinnamon; cook, turning frequently. Cover pan for a few minutes to soften apples; remove cover. Cook a little longer until it has a rich glaze; place on platter with sausages. Serve hot with toast, muffins, pancakes or waffles, making as many as needed.

Kentucky Scramble

1 C. whole kernel corn, fresh, canned or frozen
3 T. butter, or bacon drippings
1 medium green pepper, chopped
Few sprigs parsley, chopped
1 T. chopped pimento   6 eggs
1 t. salt   1/4 t. pepper

Drain corn; saute in butter or bacon drippings several minutes. Stir in green pepper, pimento and parsley; cook 5 minutes more. Beat eggs, salt and pepper together; just before serving scramble with corn mixture until set but still a little moist. Serves 4 hungry people.

Stir-Fried Asparagus

1-1/2 lbs. asparagus
1/2 C. chicken stock
1 t. salt
2 T. soy sauce
1 t. sugar
1 T. peanut oil
1 t. cornstarch, optional

This next old-time recipe is a real stir fry but was not called as such.

Asparagus lovers, like myself, relish it anytime of the year, although I seem to have a special longing for the fresh home-grown asparagus that is now in our gardens and markets. Here is a tasty way to prepare it.

Trim tough ends of asparagus; cut in diagonal sections 1-inch in length. Cook in boiling water 2 to 4 minutes; cool by running under cold water, draining well. Combine stock, salt, soy sauce, sugar and peanut oil in skillet or wok; stir-fry asparagus in mixture 1 minute, adding cornstarch for thickening if desired. To make thickening, add 2 T. water to cornstarch; mix well before adding to stir fry. Makes 6 servings.

Father's Day

Thinking of Father's Day brings back fond memories of my own father, and I have discovered that good fathers never really leave us. My father is very close to me now and he departed from this world more than 35 years ago. One of my first memories of my father was when I would go down to the barn to meet him so I could walk back to the house with him for dinner at noon, hand in hand. I remember thinking about how big his hand was. He must have been nine feet tall.

Papa wore his farmer's overalls all week; he had only one suit of clothes that he wore to church on Sundays. Yet, to my thinking now, he was a real gentleman.

I recall walking along the sidewalk in town with him when he reminded me that a lady always walked on the inside—the man next to the curb. He also said that a lady always offers her hand when she meets a man if she wants to shake hands; it is her choice. When I was older he double-checked my dating habits, which all good fathers do, and all teenagers resent at the time. I knew that he always expected me to be what he called a "lady."

Then I ponder about our forefathers. I like to think of the men and their families who caught the "Michigan Fever" and came with thousands of others to settle in Michigan in the 1830s. My father was born only 40 years after Michigan became a state, just a pinpoint in the history of time. We think of our fathers as old men with long white beards; that was not the way it was during the settlement of Michigan. The pioneers of Michigan were the nation's youth searching for homes.

The 1840 federal census for Michigan states these surprising facts: the classification of "Twenty and under Thirty" was the largest in any grouping; the second largest was under 5 years of age; it was predominantly a male population; to appreciate the extreme youth of the pioneers we need to know that 54% of the population was under 20 and 75% less than 30 years of age. One can imagine the robust appetites of those hardy young men! It must have kept their wives "hopping." Potatoes, beans, cornbread and molasses cake were favorites. Papa loved puddings, apple pie and pancakes with fresh side pork or sausage. Here are a couple of recipes loved by our young fathers of today.

Old-Fashioned Baked Beans *(Made the easy way)*

1 (1 lb. 5 oz.) can pork and beans
2 T. good quality tomato catsup

3 T. brown sugar
2 strips bacon, diced

Stir together first three ingredients in bean pot of 1-qt. casserole. Top with bacon and bake uncovered at 350 for 45 to 60 minutes. Makes 4 servings.

Frozen Peanut Butter Pie

1 (8-oz.) package cream cheese, softened
1 (14 oz.) can sweetened condensed milk
3/4 C. peanut butter
2 T. lemon juice concentrate
1 t. vanilla extract

1 C. whipping cream, whipped, or
  one (4 oz.) container of non-dairy
  frozen whipped topping, thawed
Chocolate fudge ice cream topping
Chocolate Crunch Crust (below)

Filling:

In large mixing bowl, beat cheese until fluffy; gradually beat in sweetened condensed milk, and the peanut butter, until smooth. Stir in lemon juice and vanilla. Fold in whipped cream. Turn into prepared crust; drizzle topping over pie. Freeze 4 hours.

Chocolate Crunch Crust:

In heavy saucepan, over low heat melt 1/2 cup margarine or butter and one 6-oz. package of chocolate chips. Remove from heat, gently stir in 2-1/2 C. oven-toasted rice cereal, until completely coated. Press on bottom and up sides of a buttered 9 or 10 inch pie pan. Chill 30 minutes.

This pie can be made with a graham cracker crust also; however, this chocolate crust is "Out of this world."

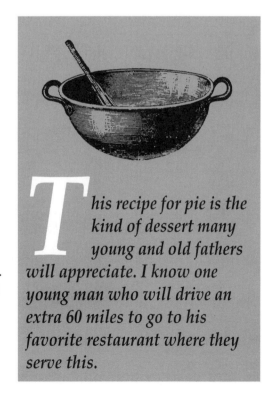

*T*his recipe for pie is the kind of dessert many young and old fathers will appreciate. I know one young man who will drive an extra 60 miles to go to his favorite restaurant where they serve this.

Summer

We could say "Every day's a Holiday" because we live in the Great Lakes basin. Even though we work hard in our shops, offices and farms, we still find the time for summer fun and relaxation.

From the Fourth of July to Labor Day we make the very best use of every day. If we are not on the golf courses or beaches, we could be out on scenic roads along with the antique cars. When the antique car drivers meet in our town every August, it's a real celebration.

Summer is company time, family reunion time, carnivals, boating, fishing or just idling away an afternoon on the patio or under a shady tree. We might even be out picking berries or cherries.

There are always special meals to prepare and we like to do it the easy way. No matter how much we love to cook, we still do not want to spend a gorgeous summer day in the kitchen. Here are some happy summer cooking ideas.

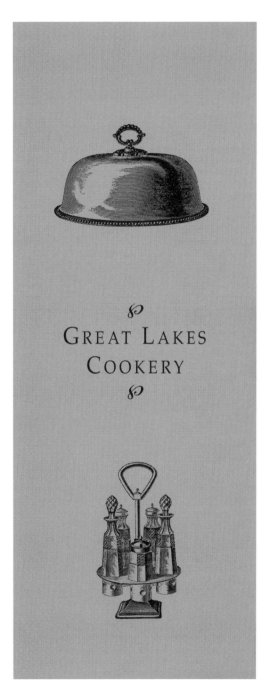

ᔥ
GREAT LAKES
COOKERY
ᔥ

Fourth of July— Strawberry Shortcake

Mother never served a small strawberry shortcake; she made a big "batch" when the home-grown berries were ripe. It was a real treat for our family because we did not have them shipped in from the south then. We had to wait for the home-grown variety. It was practically a family tradition to have a strawberry shortcake on the Fourth of July.

The wild strawberries grew best along the railroad tracks about a mile from our farm. We never had enough of them to make a shortcake. In fact, we usually had eaten most of those luscious morsels before we reached home. How I loved those berries and I could easily relate to that boy in the poem we memorized in school.

Barefoot Boy

Blessing on thee, little man
Barefoot Boy with cheeks of tan
With red lips, redder still
Kissed by strawberries
On the hill

I can imagine how happily the first settlers of our country welcomed the wild strawberries, especially after a long winter of beans, codfish, corn meal and salt pork which was the main diet for settlers in New England.

From <u>Annals of America</u>: Francis Higginson wrote in 1629 that "diverse and excellent potherbs grow abundantly among the grass, as strawberry leaves in all places of the country, and plenty of strawberries in their time."

Maybe they are as old as time.

Old-Fashioned Strawberry Shortcake

Follow this recipe for baking powder biscuits.
Mix and sift:

2 C. flour   4 t. baking powder
a pinch of salt

It's O.K. to add about 1 T. sugar here if you wish. Work in 4 T. shortening with the fingertips. Add 2/3 to 3/4 C. milk and mix to a soft dough. Pat out on a slightly floured board. Cut with a large round cutter. Bake in hot oven 425 degrees for 10 to 15 minutes. Split open while hot and spread on a lot of butter. Pour crushed sweetened strawberries between the layers and on the top. Serve while warm with heavy cream.

*H*ow can one improve on the strawberry itself? Perhaps with this special jam for "year-round" pleasure. Here is the modern way to make:

Strawberry-Rhubarb Jam

2 C. prepared fruit (about 1 pt. fully ripe strawberries and 1 lb. red stalked rhubarb)
4 C. sugar   3/4 C. water
1 box pectin

Prepare the fruit. Stem and thoroughly crush one layer at a time, about 1 pint strawberries. Measure 1 C. into large bowl or pan. Cut about 1 lb. rhubarb into 2-inch pieces and finely grind. Measure 1 C. and add to the strawberries.

To make the jam:

Thoroughly mix sugar into fruit; let stand 10 minutes. Mix water and fruit pectin in a small saucepan. Bring to a full boil and boil 1 minute, stirring constantly. Stir into fruit. Continue stirring 3 minutes (a few sugar crystals will remain). Ladle quickly into scalded containers. Cover at once with tight lids. Let stand at room temperature 24 hours; store in freezer. Small amounts can be covered and stored in refrigerator up to 3 weeks.

Strawberry-Rhubarb Pie (Pie crust for a two-crust pie)

Filling:
1-1/2 C. rhubarb cut in 1-inch pieces
1 pt. strawberries, crushed or sliced
1-1/2 C. sugar (just one C. if strawberries are sweet)
2 T. flour

Mix the above ingredients and put into an unbaked pie shell. Dot with a little butter and cover with top crust. A lattice crust is beautiful with this pie. Bake at 450 degrees 15 minutes, then lower heat to 350. Bake until crust is golden brown and the fruit bubbles up in the center.

Melon Stack-Up

Cut chilled honeydew melon into 1/2-inch thick slices. Peel and place on individual dessert plates. Sprinkle with lemon or lime juice. Fill centers with softened cream cheese mixed with sliced strawberries; add some sliced banana. Garnish with a whole berry.

Then there is this "Lickin good" strawberry-rhubarb pie. Rhubarb is at its best when the strawberries ripen and they really complement each other.

Strawberries are so good; they do not need a lot of fancy fixings, and are beautiful enough to make any dessert very special. Just try this easy fruit medley when you don't have the time or the desire to cook.

*H**ere is a delicious strawberry recipe you can make year-round, a tasty coffee cake using your favorite biscuit mix.*

Strawberry Coffee Cake

2 C. biscuit mix   1/2 C. sugar
1 egg   1/2 C. milk
1/3 C. strawberry jam

Add sugar to mix; beat egg in milk; combine mixtures. Pour in buttered pan; swirl jam over top with spoon. Bake at 425 degrees for 30 minutes until tester comes out clean when inserted in center. No matter how you fix them, strawberries are beautiful. Enjoy.

Indians Made Good Use of Wild Berries

The early settlers of Michigan found many berries growing wild. The Indians made good use of those berries, drying them for winter use. Whole tribes, men, women and children took trips to the cranberry marshes, blueberry swamps, and to openings where blackberry and raspberry bushes thrived.

My Grandmother, who was raised on a farm in the Flint area, told about the Indians coming after berries from their village near Frankenmuth. Many writers tell of dried berries that were the main winter fruit for Indians and settlers alike before orchards were planted.

In Michigan, huckleberries or blueberries grew profusely in the ashes of the forest fires. A railroad that ran from Flint to Fostoria was called the Huckleberry Line. My Mother remembers people from Flint taking the Huckleberry early in the morning to the marshes around Otter Lake and other places where the wild berries grew. They rode home with their pails full on the late train in the evening. I see now that they have made that railroad line a tourist attraction. How times change!

We do not have to work so hard to get our berries now, nor do we have to dry them for future use. We have our beautiful frozen and canned berries all year. However, I still like to preserve the fresh taste in homemade jams and jellies, going strictly by the directions on the pectin bottles or packages.

Layered Cream Cheese and Blueberries

1-1/2 C. crushed round buttery crackers
1/4 C. butter or margarine, melted
1 pkg. (8 oz.) cream cheese, softened
2 T. sugar
2 T. milk
1-1/2 C. blueberries, halved strawberries or raspberries
1 pkg. (4 oz.) instant pudding, vanilla or lemon
1-1/2 C. cold milk
1-3/4 C. non-dairy whipped topping

Combine crackers and butter and press into bottom of 8-inch square pan. Chill. Beat cream cheese with sugar and 2 T. milk in bowl until smooth. Spread evenly in crumb-lined pan. Arrange berries on cream cheese mixture. Prepare pudding mix with 1-1/2 C. milk as directed on package for pie filling. Fold in 1/2 C. of whipped topping.

Spoon over berries and chill until set, about 2 hours. Garnish with remaining whipped topping and additional berries if desired.

Cut in squares to serve 9.

The next two recipes can be made with strawberries, blueberries or raspberries.

Mother served her blueberries with fresh cream and sugar, yet my daughter and I discovered that we like a bowl of frozen blueberries with a little 2% milk poured over them while they are still frozen. We used a sugar substitute when we were on a special diet; now we eat berries this way even when we are not on the diet.

This next recipe would be just as beautiful made with raspberries. You might want to sweeten them a little. This dessert is like shortcake plus.

What problems those young people had in the old days! Cherry pie still might be a way to a young man's heart—or the heart of a man of any age. No matter how it is made, with those fresh tart cherries and a rich homemade crust with lots of sugar the way Mother made it, with the prepared packaged crust and canned cherry pie filling or fresh frozen ones, they are all good. You can't miss!

Strawberry Cake

1 pound cake
1 pint strawberries, hulled   1/2 C. sugar
1 pkg. (8 oz.) cream cheese, softened
1-3/4 C. non-dairy whipped topping

Cut cake horizontally into 3 layers. Crush 1-1/2 C. of the berries, reserving remaining berries for garnish. Add sugar to cream cheese, beating until smooth. Fold in topping, then fold in crushed berries. Fill and frost cake with cream cheese mixture. Garnish with berries and chill.

Cherries Are Ripe

Cherries are ripe, and what a glorious season for us cherry lovers! The very thought of those luscious, bright red cherries fills me with enough ambition to make a cherry pie, even if the temperature is way up there. The writer of this old song must have been a cherry lover from way back.

Can she bake a cherry pie?
Billy Boy, Billy Boy,
Can she bake a cherry pie?
Charming Billy,
She can bake a cherry pie
Quick as a cat can wink its eye
But she's a sweet young thing
And cannot leave her mother.

Cherry Pie Crust

2 C. flour, stirred but not sifted
1/4 t. salt
3/4 C. vegetable shortening
About 1/4 C. ice water

Mix the flour and salt. Cut in the shortening (one of those shortening blenders works well for this); however, I have used two knives for years. Then add the ice water a little at a time and blend in. The old-time pie makers all say to use the water as if it was gold, very sparingly. Using your hands, form dough into two balls and roll out between sheets of waxed paper.

*F*rom an old yellowed recipe card, I find my tried and true directions for cherry pie.

Cherry Pie Filling

Use a heaping quart box of cherries, pit them, or one can of tart cherries can be used. Add 1 C. sugar (1-1/4 C. if your family has a sweet tooth), and 2-1/2 T. minute tapioca. Let the above ingredients stand while you are making the crust. Bake 15 minutes at 400 degrees then lower to 350. When it bubbles in the center it is done, about 40 minutes all together.

Apple Cherry Pie

Use the preceding crust or your favorite crust mix for this pie. Mix 1 T. flour, 1 C. sugar, 1/2 t. allspice, 1/2 t. nutmeg and 2 T. maraschino cherry syrup. Sprinkle 1/2 C. in a 9-inch unbaked pastry shell. Add 4 C. pared and sliced tart apples; sprinkle with remaining sugar mixture. Dot with butter or margarine. Cover with pastry strips, lattice-style; flute edge, bake in hot oven, 425 degrees, 40 to 45 minutes.

or a special occasion you can make this:

Creamy Cherry-Pecan Pie

1 can cherry pie filling
2 T. brown sugar
1/4 t. cinnamon
1/4 C. chopped pecans
1 baked 9-inch pie shell or graham cracker crumb crust, cooled
1 pkg. (4-serving size) vanilla-flavored instant pudding and 1/2 C. thawed whipped topping

Combine cherry pie filling, sugar, cinnamon, and nuts. Spread half in pie shell; chill remaining cherry mixture. Prepare pie or pudding mix according to directions on the box. Fold in the whipped topping. Spoon over cherry mixture in the shell. Freeze 1 hour or chill 3 hours before serving. Garnish with reserved cherry mixture; add additional whipped topping if desired.

Corn On The Cob

Corn: The color and taste of summer. What is more beautiful than those green acres of tall corn growing everywhere in our Great Lakes area? It is said that if you listen hard enough you can hear it grow. Those delicious ears of golden corn on our picnic or dinner table also make a perfect picture of America's bounteous harvest.

Corn or maize is the only important cereal of American origin and U.S. hybrids make it the most productive of all grains. Indians introduced corn-on-the-cob to the pilgrims. I wonder how they cooked it. Most likely they were roasted over an open fire. We can evoke the past and yet use modern simplicity when preparing and serving corn. The main thing to remember when cooking fresh corn is do not overcook.

Corn-On-The-Cob #1

"Strip the husks and silk from ears of freshly pulled corn. The sooner corn is eaten after being gathered, the sweeter it is. Steam in a steamer for 20 minutes, or boil 10 minutes. In either case serve soon, each ear wrapped in a small napkin. To roast, lay on a gridiron over a clear but now fierce fire, turning over a little at a time as the surface becomes browned; time about 25 minutes. Wrap in a napkin and eat with butter, salt and pepper, the same as boiled corn. The napkin is used to protect the fingers from the heat. Serve as a separate course." (I do not believe they had paper napkins at that time.)

The following is from "Catering for Two," published in 1898.

Corn-On-The-Cob #2

4 ears of corn

Place unhusked ears of corn directly on floor of oven, leaving space in between. Microwave on high, uncovered, 15 to 19 minutes. Let stand 5 minutes. To remove husk, grasp corn at base of ear, using napkin to protect hand. With free hand, back at tip, gradually pull husk at tip of ear, allowing steam to escape before stripping off rest of husk. Remove silk by grasping firmly with hand or by brushing away with napkin. Makes 4 servings. (I do this with just one ear of corn and microwave just under 5 minutes. The corn is always cooked just the right amount.)

This is the way that I fix corn-on-the-cob. It's from my microwave cookbook.

The old books all have recipes for corn pudding and I know that they were delicious. Here is a modern version of the old favorite. Use the freshest corn possible—the juicier the better.

I made this recipe and I could not believe how very delicious it was. It was as light as a feather and beautiful to see. I made it with corn from the supermarket that was not home-grown, so this could be made anytime you can buy fresh corn. The cutting of the kernels and scraping was a little time-consuming but not difficult, and well worth the effort. I will make this pudding again and again. You may notice that no milk is used, just the delicious juice of the corn. I used to make corn fritters. My family loved them. You can use the canned or fresh frozen for the following.

Fresh Corn Pudding

6-8 ears of fresh corn, enough for 3 cups pulp
2 eggs, separated   2 t. sugar
3 T. butter or margarine 1 t. salt

Slit down center of corn kernels with sharp knife. Press out pulp and juice into bowl, using a dull-edged knife; add egg yolks, sugar, salt and 2 T. of melted butter. Beat the egg whites until stiff peaks form; fold in corn mixture. Turn into greased shallow 1-quart baking dish; dot with remaining butter. Bake in 350 degree oven 45 minutes or until golden brown. Makes 6 servings.

Corn Fritters

1/2 C. flour   1/2 t. salt
1/2 t. baking powder
1 egg, beaten   1/2 C. milk
1 T. butter or margarine, melted
1 can (2 C.) creamed corn, drained, or 1 can whole kernel corn, drained

Sift flour, baking powder and salt together, add egg, butter and milk; then add flour and corn. Drop by spoonfuls onto griddle like pancakes, using vegetable oil with a little butter for flavor. Fry until golden brown on both sides and serve with pancake syrup or honey.

Our Summer Melons

Years ago watermelon time meant that the older boys in most farm neighborhoods went out after dark to steal one or two. They did not consider it too wrong; they bragged about it to the younger children. It was the only thing we heard of being stolen in our innocent time. Sweet juicy watermelons were a great temptation.

Both watermelons and muskmelons have been cultivated for many centuries. It is possible that they were not all perfect specimens. A Spanish writer of 1513 recognized the extremes of quality in the muskmelon and said, "If it is bad it is a bad thing; we are wont to say that the good are like good women, and the bad like bad women."

All melons are at their best now so let's serve them often, the most natural and delicious of desserts. They contribute to the real joy of eating. Melons of every kind are perfect for picnics; they come in their own containers and you do not need to carry anything home.

I am happy to say that the melons sold at our supermarket can be counted on to be good. I have recently enjoyed the honeydews, which are really muskmelons. My old National Geographic states that all cantaloupes are muskmelons, but not all muskmelons are cantaloupes. Confusing? Melons are very ancient, native to Persia (Iran) and nearby countries.

Watermelons are so ancient, the culture goes back to pre-historic times. They have been discovered growing wild in Central Africa from where it is believed they originated. David Livingston found large tracts literally covered with watermelons. Even today in semi-desert districts they are grown for an important source of water during dry spells. The watermelon culture has spread around the world; beer is made from it in Russia, Americans make watermelon wine, and the Chinese preserve it in brine.

*I*f you are serving luncheon to the girls, they will welcome melon with assorted cheeses and crackers; the honeydews are special for this. For an extra special dessert you can make the following recipe.

*T*here is something magnificent about melon desserts. Add melon balls or cubes to any fruit and pour this sauce over all.

Molded Melon Medley

1 pkg. (3 oz.) strawberry-flavored gelatin
1 C. hot water
1/2 C. apricot liquid plus 1/2 C. juice from the fresh melon
1-1/2 to 2 C. fresh melon balls
1 can (9 oz.) apricots, drained and sliced
Fresh red or green grapes (about 1 C.)

Dissolve gelatin in hot water. Add the apricot liquid and melon juice; chill for about 10 minutes. Add the melon balls, apricots and grapes. Pour into individual molds or in a square pan to set. Cut in squares or unmold onto salad greens. Very pretty and tasty.

Fresh Fruit Topping

1/2 C. pineapple juice
1/4 C. lemon juice
2 eggs, well beaten
3/4 C. sugar
3/4 pint heavy whipping cream

In a double boiler, mix juices together; add well-beaten eggs and sugar and cook until thickened. Cool and chill in refrigerator. Whip cream and fold into cooled fruit mixture. Serve over fresh fruit. Makes 6 servings.

Melon Salad

1 cantaloupe, peeled
leaf lettuce
2 C. watermelon balls
1-1/2 C. honeydew balls
Sprig of mint (garnish)
3/4 C. Sherry Mayonnaise (recipe follows)

Slice the cantaloupe into rings about an inch thick and remove seeds. (The cantaloupe will be easier to peel if sliced first.) Place on lettuce on salad plates.

Fill each ring with watermelon and honeydew balls. Garnish with mint if you wish. Serve with the following:

Sherry Mayonnaise

1 C. mayonnaise
1/4 C. pale dry sherry
1 C. whipping cream

Mix all together. That's all, and it is elegant.

This next salad uses three different melons; the contrast in color and texture is beautiful.

Cool Cookin'

Summer cooking is much easier than it was in Grandmother's time. She no doubt used a three-burner oil stove in the back kitchen—or a porch-like room called the summer kitchen. It was a real challenge to regulate those oil burners. She could bake a pie or a pudding in the small oven that she set on top of the burners. However, she built a fire in the big wood range once a week to bake her bread. She also did most of her other baking that same day. No matter how hot the day, the bread must be baked.

Those oil burners also were used on wash day to heat the water in the copper boiler—like those we now see in the antique shops. I can still see Mother shaving the P&G or Fels Naptha soap into the boiling water. I am sure that my great grandmother and possibly my grandmother made their own soap. I remember that Mother made some during World War II. It was a good serviceable soap for general cleaning but very hard on the hands. Mother could buy the lye to make her soap then, but our grandmothers had to make their own lye from hardwood ashes.

My goodness, I am rambling on, away from the subject of summer cooking. I recall the first time I read "A Lantern In Her Hand" by Bess Streeter Aldrich. It was and still is one of my favorite books. She describes the pioneering days in Nebraska and tells how the neighborhood was shocked when someone brought potato salad to a party. "Imagine eating cold potatoes," they said. The old-timers thought all vegetables should be cooked and served hot. We've come a long way, haven't we? Cold salads and entrees of all kinds are popular now. The old neighborhood would no doubt be more surprised if they were served this dish.

Rice Salad

1 C. cooked rice, chilled	1/8 C. raisins
1/8 C. ham, chopped	2 t. carrot, grated
2 t. orange peel, grated	
2 t. almonds, chopped	
1 t. orange juice or salad dressing	

This much will serve 2. Toss all ingredients together, mixing well. Serve on lettuce or surround by sprigs of mint.

Vinaigrette Dressing

1/4 C. vegetable oil
1/4 C. white wine vinegar
1/4 t. lemon peel, grated
Dash tarragon
Salt and pepper to taste

Mix well and store in a covered container. Keep chilled.

Chilled Cucumber Soup

Here is a salad dressing recipe that is perfect for this salad, sliced tomatoes or any leafy vegetable.

We are even eating chilled soups; here is a tasty one.

1 large cucumber	1/2 clove garlic, mashed
Dash of pepper	Dash of lemon juice
2 C. plain yogurt	A few dill or mint leaves

Peel, seed and shred cucumber and mix with garlic, pepper, lemon and yogurt. Taste and adjust seasoning. If too thick, add a little cold milk. Keep well chilled. Serves 2.

We should have a potato salad recipe. This is more modern, I am sure, than the one served on a farm in Nebraska in the 1880s.

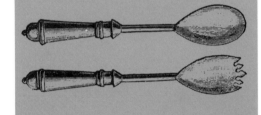

Now, for our no-cook dessert. Paula McGinnis served this at our Historical Society meeting and it was delicious.

Chunky Ham Potato Salad

2 medium potatoes, cooked and sliced
2 T. Italian salad dressing
1 T. snipped parsley
1 can chunk ham, flaked with fork
2 C. salad greens (lettuce, spinach, romaine, etc.) torn into bite size pieces
3 hard-cooked eggs, quartered
3/4 C. Swiss cheese strips
1/2 C. ripe olives, pitted and sliced
1/4 C. green onion, chopped
1/4 C. Italian salad dressing

In bowl, sprinkle potatoes with 2 tablespoons of salad dressing and parsley. Cover and marinate in the refrigerator for several hours or overnight. Layer remaining ingredients. Just before serving, pour 1/2 C. Italian dressing over salad and toss lightly. Makes 4 servings.

Paula's Dessert

Graham Cracker Crumb Crust for a 9-inch pie shell
1-1/2 C. graham cracker crumbs
1/4 C. sugar
1/3 C. margarine

Mix all together until crumbly and form a crust in the pie pan. Paula bakes hers just five minutes at 375 degrees. When shell is cooked, make the filling.

FILLING:

1 pkg. (8 oz.) cream cheese, softened at room temperature
1 can (14 oz.) condensed milk
1 t. vanilla
1/2 C. fresh lemon juice

Beat the softened cream cheese and the condensed milk until smooth, then add the lemon juice and vanilla. Pour into the cool shell. Put a few more cracker crumbs on top for garnish and chill until firm. (Paula put a spoonful of fresh sugared strawberries on top of each serving of this delicious dessert.)

Posh Squash

2 lb. yellow squash, sliced
1 C. mayonnaise
1 small onion, chopped   2 eggs, beaten
1/2 t. salt   1/4 t. pepper
1 C. (8 oz.) Parmesan cheese, grated
1/2 C. soft bread crumbs
1 T. margarine or butter, melted

Cook squash in boiling water to cover, 10 to 15 minutes or until tender. Drain and cool slightly. Combine mayonnaise, onion, eggs, salt and pepper. Stir until well blended. Add squash, stirring gently. Pour into a lightly greased 1-1/2 qt. casserole. Combine cheese, bread crumbs and butter; spoon over casserole and bake at 350 for 30 minutes.

Squash Can Be Posh

We have the privilege of buying squash year-round and sometimes I think that we bypass it, taking it for granted. However, now is the time to make the most of the abundant fresh ones at the market or in our gardens.

First comes summer squash, including yellow crook-neck, straight neck and zucchini and those delicious cymblings from the south. These squashes originated in Central America and were grown by the Indians all over our country. They were planted in Europe in 1500s. They are the kind that must be picked and eaten before they ripen and the shells become hard. Many of them need as little as four days of growing time after they develop from the flowers, so watch for them in the garden to enjoy them at their best. These squashes are called vegetable marrows in all countries except in the United States.

Here are a couple of recipes for summer squash. Use the kind you have on hand in these recipes.

Dilly Squash

1 lb. yellow summer squash
2 T. butter or margarine
1 T. fresh parsley, snipped

1/4 t. dill weed
1/4 t. salt
Dash of onion powder

Slice squash. Melt butter in skillet, add squash and all the other ingredients. Cover and cook over low heat 8 to 10 minutes or until tender, stirring occasionally. Serve piping hot.

Following closely in our gardens, even before the early summer squash are gone, are the wonderful butter squashes: butternut, buttercup and acorn. Some people say the butternut is their favorite, others like the buttercup best, yet almost everyone likes those little acorns. They are easy to fill with meat or vegetables, with a little honey or maple syrup for sweetening. This next recipe is a little different, using onions and light molasses.

Glazed Squash

3 medium acorn squash
2 C. small onions, cooked or canned, drained
1/2 C. walnut meats, broken

1/3 C. butter or margarine, melted
1/3 C. light molasses
1/4 t. salt
1/4 t. cinnamon

Cut squash in half lengthwise; remove seeds. Bake cut-side down in a shallow baking pan in moderate oven (350 degrees) 35 to 40 minutes or until almost tender. Turn squash cut-side up and sprinkle with salt. Fill with onions and walnuts. Combine remaining ingredients; spoon over squash and filling. Continue baking 15 to 20 minutes or until tender, brushing occasionally with sauce in pan to glaze. Serve this with thick slices of rye bread for a real tasty meal. Makes 6 servings.

Then there are the winter squashes. I like to buy the frozen kind, doing it the easy way. If you are growing Hubbard and other hard-shelled squash, you can enjoy the true taste as we did before we had freezers. I remember my father cutting the squash with an axe and Mother baking it in large pieces in the oven—a real treat for Thanksgiving dinner.

Savory Barbecued Ribs

4 lbs. spare ribs, cracked in serving-size pieces
1 onion, peeled and quartered
2 t. salt
1/4 t. pepper

Place ribs, onion, salt and pepper in 3 quarts of water in a large kettle. Bring to a boil. Reduce heat and simmer, covered for 1-1/2 hours or until tender. Drain.

Sauce:
1/2 C. vinegar
1/2 C. light brown sugar
1/2 C. ketchup
1/4 C. chili sauce
1/4 C. Worcestershire sauce
2 T. onion, chopped
1 T. lemon juice
1/2 t. dry mustard

Combine all ingredients in medium saucepan. Simmer uncovered for one hour, stirring occasionally. This can be done while the ribs are cooking. Arrange ribs on rack in broiler pan if cooking in the broiler, or over foil with holes punched into it if over the outdoor grill. Brush with sauce. Broil about 5 inches from source of heat, basting frequently with sauce, cooking 10 minutes on each side.

Early Barbecues— Outdoors Adds Flavor

I suppose even before recorded history our ancestors were roasting meat over a fire. Charles Lamb (1775-1834) told of how roasting or broiling meat began in his "Dissertation of Roast Pig." He tells of how the Chinaman's house burned down and his pig was roasted; he touched the pig, burned his fingers and stuck them in his mouth to cool, and he discovered that "some of the crumbs of the scorched skin came away with his fingers, and for the first time in his life (in the world's life, indeed, for before him no man had known it) he tasted cracklings!"

Now, the Chinaman had to burn down his house several times to get this wonderful flavor, and soon his neighbors were doing the same thing. Fires could be seen in every direction. This custom of firing houses continued "til in process of time a sage arose who discovered that the flesh of swine, or indeed of any other animal, might be cooked (burnt, as they called it) without the necessity of burning down a house to dress it. Then began the first gridiron."

I am glad that we do not have to burn down a house to enjoy these.

Our long, long ago ancestors really started something when they discovered the tantalizing and delicious taste of meat cooked over an open fire. I still wonder why food tastes better cooked out-of-doors, even my morning cup of coffee seems to have a better flavor out on the patio. I am sure that the fresh air, even the smoke from the fire, must be good for digestive juices.

My granddaughter, Barbie and her husband, Bob, cook delicious food on their outdoor grill all year long. I love to go there for many reasons: to see my great grandson, Bobbie, to view the changing seasons from their living room windows, where two trout streams converge into one on their front lawn, and to climb the hill in back of their home, where wild flowers grow.

Not the least of these treasures is the eating of foods from their grill. Sometimes they use charcoal; however, Bob likes to use some of the fragrant wood he cuts from their property. Barbie likes to take the time to marinate meats; she said that is what really makes the difference. Here is her recipe for pork chops. She has marinated them for a couple of hours but they are much better if they marinate 12 hours or overnight.

Barbie's Pork Chops

Thick pork chops are better. Marinate in Italian salad dressing 12 hours or overnight. Grill over hot coals, 10 minutes on each side; test for doneness. That's all there is to it and they are out of this world.

My grandchildren have a system; Barbie prepares the food and Bob does the rest—getting the fire just right and doing all of the grilling. They like to fix potatoes this way.

Potatoes In Foil

Place enough sliced potatoes for each serving on square of foil, either baking potatoes or early red potatoes. Peel or scrub and slice. Put slices of onion on potatoes, sprinkling with salt and pepper; add pat of butter on top. Wrap tightly; cook on grill.

Barbie says that if you want them crispy, lay directly on coals a little while. Check them so they do not burn. Open one package to see if potatoes are tender. Serve.

This next recipe calls for fresh fish, but you can use the thawed fish fillets from the frozen food section of the supermarket. You will be delighted with the flavor and texture.

Fish Fillets In Foil

Fish fillets   Chopped onion
Butter   Lemon juice
Salt and pepper to taste

Prepare as for individual servings of potatoes; cook on grill. Turn over; it does not take long to cook fish; check one package after 10 minutes. It is done when it flakes easily with fork.

Then there is Bob's barbecue sauce. He says that this sauce is good on everything: hamburgers, hot dogs, kabobs and country-style ribs.

Bob's Special Barbecue Sauce

7 oz. barbecue sauce
1/2 C. pancake syrup
1/2 stick margarine or butter

Cook all ingredients to melt butter; mix well. Use to brush on favorite meat.

Bob and Barbie both agree that when they have a good juicy steak, they skip all of the decorations. All one needs is the steak itself grilled to each one's choice of doneness.

Picnics – People Main Ingredient

The first ingredient for a good picnic is a group of happy people. All picnics have a party atmosphere regardless of size. It could be a family reunion, a Sunday school or last-day-of-school picnic, a small group of friends who just love to be out of doors, or a picnic for two where the "jug of wine, a loaf of bread and thou" are the only necessary ingredients.

No matter what kind of picnic we are planning, the north country is the perfect place for it. Our northern seasons beckon us to the parks, woods, lakes or sand dunes. Before we moved north we always vacationed in Northern Michigan, thinking that if we came early enough in the spring or late enough in the fall, we would miss the mosquitoes. How mistaken we were. They were always there to greet us. However, we doused ourselves with citronella and had our picnics anyway.

So round up a few friends and plan a picnic. Since I live alone, I have learned to enjoy almost everything by myself; however, a picnic means company. Sometimes when I go for a walk in our State Park I put an apple in my coat pocket—almost as good as a picnic.

Picnics are easier to prepare now than they have ever been. We can stop at the fast food place and buy a healthy, beautiful salad and sandwiches, though it is fun to cook your own hot dogs or hamburgers.

Here is a salad to make and have on hand just in case a picnic comes up. My daughter enjoyed this at her office picnic and her host, Jack, copied the recipe for me. It is similar to others that are popular salads this season. This recipe sounds easy—no definite amount—so make it so it tastes just the way you like it.

This next cheese spread would be welcome on any picnic. It will give it a real party flavor. Serve this while the fire is heating to the perfect stage to grill the hamburgers, hot dogs or fish.

Broccoli Salad

2 small-size bunches fresh broccoli, chopped
1 lb. bacon, fried and crumbled
1/2 box raisins
Mayonnaise or salad dressing

Add mayonnaise or salad dressing and mix together. The longer it marinates, the better it tastes.

Spirited Cheese Spread

1/2 lb. sharp Cheddar cheese
1/2 pkg. sharp Cheddar cheese food
1 pkg. (8 oz.) Neufchatel or cream cheese
1 stick margarine
1/4 C. brandy
1 t. curry powder
1 T. Worcestershire sauce
5 drops Tabasco

Grate first two cheeses. Combine with other ingredients in food processor until smooth. Refrigerate several hours to allow flavors to blend. Serve on low-sodium crackers. Note: When given a choice between Neufchatel or cream cheese, remember that the Neufchatel has less butter fat and more sodium.

Just a note about hamburgers: When you form the patties, and it's a good idea to do this before you leave home, mix about one teaspoon of Creole seasoning into 1 pound of meat. It makes very tasty hamburgers. Don't forget the fresh fruits, pickles and any other goodies in the refrigerator, especially big dill pickles.

Applesauce Raisin Cake

2-1/2 C. flour	1 egg, beaten
1t. baking soda	1 C. molasses
1 t. cinnamon	1 C. applesauce
1/2 t. salt	1/2 C. raisins
1/2 C. margarine	

4 t. lemon juice
3/4 C. sifted powdered sugar

In a medium bowl combine flour, soda, cinnamon and salt. Cut in butter or margarine to resemble coarse crumbs. In another small bowl stir together egg, molasses and applesauce; blend into flour mixture just until moistened. Stir in raisins. Turn into a greased and floured 9 x 9 x 2-inch baking pan. Bake at 350 degrees for 40 to 45 minutes or until cake tests done. Cool in pan 15 minutes. Combine powdered sugar and lemon juice; spread over warm cake. Serve warm or cool.

Happy Picnicking!

We all like dessert on a picnic. The fresh air whets our appetites. You might stop at the bakery or bake your favorite cookies or brownies. They are so good with fruit – a must at picnics.

If you want to make a cake, this next recipe is a delicious quickie. You most likely will have everything on the pantry shelf for it and you do not even need your mixer. It will be easy to carry because you just leave it in the baking pan. The molasses and applesauce give it a sweet, old-time flavor.

Tomatoes

In my genealogical research, I came across an account about "The Year Without a Summer."

The year of 1816 in New York state was one of disaster, for it was claimed that it froze every month of the year. It is called the year of two winters. Famine existed in some places that had crop failure the year before. It is told that people crossed over a bridge of ice on Cayuga Lake in June when there was six inches of snow on the ground. It is also reported that on the Fourth of July there was ice of considerable thickness on the lake. Song birds froze to death, covering the ground under evergreen trees, and many young animals perished in the cold.

This made me wonder how our forefathers made it through those kinds of conditions. Grandma's garden was more than a hobby; it was necessary for their survival, their way of life. She had to make good use of everything grown as soon as it matured. They had to use their tomatoes as they ripened, so many were canned for future use. They did not make spaghetti and taco sauces, though they made lots of chili sauce and chow-chow from the ripe and green tomatoes. They broiled, sauteed, and scalloped them. Here are a few recipes from an old cookbook (1908). These recipes are just as good now as they were so many years ago.

Sauteed Tomatoes

Slice tomatoes; season with salt and pepper. Dip in crumbs, eggs and crumbs again, and saute in hot fry pan. Serve on buttered toast. The crumbs probably should be fine, dry ones.

Buttered Tomatoes

Melt one cup butter; sprinkle six sliced tomatoes with salt and pepper. Put in chafing dish; cover and cook 20 minutes. Serve on toast. A double boiler or a covered, non-stick pan could substitute for the chafing dish.

Baked Tomatoes

From "Cooking by Touch"
4 tomato halves
6 T. Dijon mustard
3 T. finely chopped green onions
1/2 t. basil

Lightly salt tomatoes and drain on paper towels. Preheat oven to 425 degrees. Mix remaining ingredients together. Spread over tomatoes; place them in lightly-greased pan. Bake in a 425 degree oven 10 minutes.

Be sure to serve the fresh tomatoes often during their ripening season. Our mothers always had them sliced for at least one meal a day when they were ripe, usually with sugar, salt and pepper and a cruet of vinegar on the side. We never tired of those luscious tomatoes; the season was over far too soon!

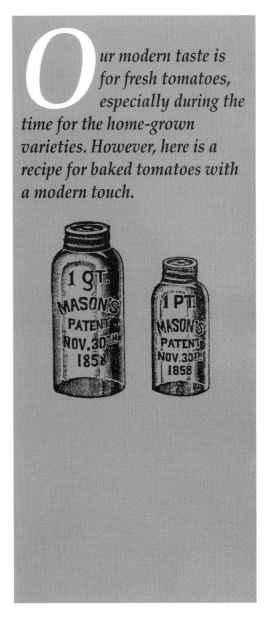

*O*ur modern taste is for fresh tomatoes, especially during the time for the home-grown varieties. However, here is a recipe for baked tomatoes with a modern touch.

Fall

Fall is the only season that needs two names to describe it. I love the word, autumn; it seems magical and even has a beautiful sound when spoken. Autumn is harvest time; the season starts with mother nature at her very best. We picture a cornucopia of pumpkins, bright leaves, and gorgeous fall vegetables and fruits with thanksgiving.

Then the leaves are gone and the poets write about the mystery of Fall. We do have those dark misty days; then one morning we awake to Indian summer. We always think that it will last, and we cannot believe that it is time to plan our Thanksgiving dinner. We are wondering when we are going to do our Christmas shopping.

Food is plentiful, the warmth of our kitchens beckons us as the cold weather sharpens our appetites. It's a good time to cook!

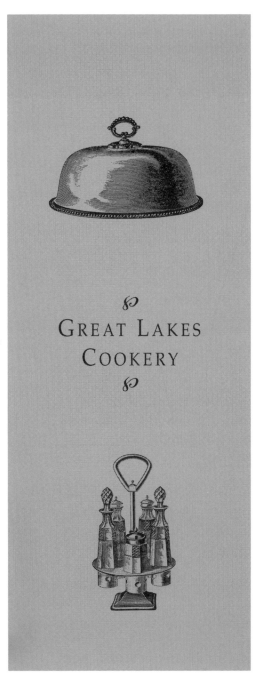

❧

GREAT LAKES
COOKERY

❧

Evening Picnics

There are so many different kinds of picnics: breakfasts, casuals, late-minute picnics when we stop for cheese, lunch meat, pop or wine on the way, also family reunions and cookouts where the fish just caught are fried.

Then there are evening picnics for those who have busy days. I recall one glorious evening; it was almost dark when we built our fire and roasted wieners and heated up baked beans. If you plan an evening picnic, it is a good idea to go before the hunting season. We heard bird calls at sunset and pheasants flew over. I still remember that picnic after many years. I hope my children and grandchildren can experience such an evening—just sitting on a log with a blanket over their shoulders in front of a fire, singing the old songs and eating grapes and apples for dessert.

Then there are times on the patio at home, where many have a grill. Or take your grill to a favorite picnic spot.

I have rediscovered some good reasons for a picnic. The scenery is perfect—our northern woods are aflame with color and that pale blue haze in the early morning will become brilliant blue before noon. I become picnic-hungry just observing such a morning.

There is a crispy cool tang in the air that whets our appetites. This is so very welcome after our hot summer days. The robins are congregating on our lawns in large flocks, telling us they will be leaving before long. We know there will be cold days ahead, so we must make the most of these luscious, glorious early fall days.

*H*ere is a tasty way to make barbecued ribs, loved by everyone.

Lemon Grilled Ribs

Make this sauce ahead of time to have it handy.

1/2 C. water
1 chicken bouillon cube
3 T. brown sugar
1 C. pineapple juice
2 cloves garlic, minced
1/4 C. onion, minced
1/4 C. catsup
1/4 C. lemon juice
2 T. cornstarch
Salt and pepper
3 lbs. spare ribs or country-style ribs

Combine first 9 ingredients in a saucepan, and season to taste with salt and pepper. Bring to a boil, stirring well. Lower heat and simmer 5 minutes; set aside.

Cut ribs into serving-size pieces (3 or 4 ribs per person). Place ribs bone-side down on grill over slow coals. Grill about 20 minutes; turn meaty side down and cook until browned. Turn meaty side up again and grill about 20 minutes longer, brush meaty side with sauce mixture. Continue to grill without turning 20 to 30 minutes; baste occasionally. Brush sauce on both sides of ribs; let cook 2 to 3 minutes on each side. Makes 4 to 6 servings.

Summer Fruit Slaw

2 C. red grape halves
1 C. shredded zucchini
1 C. shredded cabbage
1/2 C. shredded carrots
1 medium apple, cut in strips
1/2 C. French reduced-calorie dressing
1/2 C. coarsely chopped walnuts

Combine ingredients; mix lightly. Chill. Makes six servings. 180 calories per serving.

Stuffed Luncheon Loaf

Prepare 1 package (8 oz) bread stuffing according to package directions. Add 1 can (9 oz) crushed pineapple, drained. Slice 1 can (12 oz) pork-ham luncheon loaf. Alternate meat, dressing and cling peach halves in buttered loaf pan. Bake in moderate oven 375 degrees for 20 minutes.

This salad is an attractive barbecue accompaniment that can be made the day before. Serve it in a hollowed-out cabbage head or in a bowl lined with dark green outer cabbage leaves. From Kraft Kitchens.

Sometimes we like to fix a casserole or other main dish and take it to a favorite picnic spot at the last minute. Here is such a dish.

This is the time to serve fruit for dessert. Our Great Lakes muskmelons are at their best, the apples, pears, plums and peaches are deliciously ripe, and don't forget the Concord grapes. Homemade cookies are the only accompaniment needed. If it is too hot to bake, the local bakeries have delicious cookies.

Sometimes, just baking a pie or a special dessert calls for a picnic. Pack it up with some wieners or hamburger patties and rolls and head for your favorite picnic spot. You could fry bacon and eggs for such a spontaneous picnic. I always had a large frying pan packed in a basket for just such a purpose. A good rule for picnics is to make the preparations easy and have fun!

Color Tours Work Up An Appetite

Who can stay indoors on these bright and cool, invigorating October days? I want to be out to see it all. One of the first places I am anxious to visit is one of those apple orchards where there is a cider mill—this really puts one in the harvest mood—then some antique and gift shops need to be visited.

All of this gives us a terrific appetite, so we need to have food along the way. Of course, there are the Concord grapes ripening now and apples, pears and other fruits available. However, we need some sandwiches. Tuna and egg salad sandwiches have long been family favorites. Have them made before leaving home and ready to eat, because this break in the color tour must be very simple and easy to serve—maybe from the tailgate or trunk of the car.

Carry the salad dressing in a separate container and put it on the sandwiches just before eating; that way they will not be soggy and will keep better.

Tuna and Egg Salad Sandwiches

2009
Good

1 can (7 oz.) tuna fish, well drained
2 stalks of celery, cut in 1/4-inch slices
2 hard-boiled eggs, chopped
1 large dill pickle, chopped,
    or 1/4 C. pickle relish
1/4 C. finely chopped onion
Sliced stuffed olives, optional
Chopped green peppers, if desired
salt and pepper

Combine all ingredients. Spread on bread or rolls.

Banana Bread

1-3/4 C. flour
1 C. sugar
2-1/2 t. baking powder
1 t. salt
3/4 C. Grape Nuts cereal
1 C. mashed ripe banana
1/2 C. milk
1 egg, well beaten
2 T. oil or melted shortening

I like mayonnaise dressing with this salad, so take along your favorite. A little Italian dressing peps it up a bit.

Then there are some special sandwiches made with your own homemade delicious bread, the kind that is perfect with cream cheese filling.

I like this recipe for banana bread.

Mix flour with sugar, baking powder and salt; stir in cereal. Combine banana, milk, egg and shortening; add flour mixture, stirring until all flour is moistened. Pour into greased 9 x 5-inch loaf pan. Bake at 350 degrees, 1 hour, until cake tester inserted into center comes out clean. Cool in pan 10 minutes. Remove from pan; finish cooling on rack.

Brownies are good on a picnic, so easy to eat without any fuss.

This recipe sounds complicated; however, it really does all come together. You'll be delighted. It's fun to give your friends or family something special like this. Later if they are famished before returning home, you always can stop at a fast food place for hamburgers.

Be sure to have a big thermos of coffee and cider for the children in all of us and lots of paper napkins, paper cups and small plates. I like to take as many of these trips as possible before winter sets in. Who knows, maybe I will find grandmother's old apple slicer in one of those antique shops.

Cream Cheese Brownies

1 pkg. (4 oz.) German sweet chocolate
5 T. butter or margarine, used separately
1 pkg. (3 oz.) cream cheese, softened
1 C. sugar, used separately 1 T. flour
3 eggs, used separately 1-1/2 t. vanilla
1/2 t. baking powder 1/4 t. salt
1/2 C. coarsely-chopped nuts
1/2 C. flour

Melt chocolate and 3 T. butter in small saucepan over very low heat, stirring constantly; cool. Blend remaining butter with cheese until softened; gradually add 1/4 C. sugar, beating well. Blend in 1 egg, 1 T. flour and 1/2 t. vanilla. Set aside.

Beat remaining 2 eggs until thick and light in color; gradually add remaining 3/4 C. sugar, beating until thickened. Add baking powder, salt, and 1/2 C. flour; blend in cooled chocolate mixture, nuts and 1 t. vanilla. Spread half of chocolate batter into 8- or 9-inch square pan. Add cheese mixture, spreading evenly. Top with tablespoons of remaining chocolate batter. Zigzag spatula through batter to marble. Bake at 350 degrees 35 to 40 minutes until top springs back when lightly pressed in center; cool. Cut into bars or squares. Makes 16 or 20 luscious brownies.

Joe's Baked Squash

He had one large acorn squash cut into quarters and seeded. He seasoned the pieces with a little salt and put them around the beef roast in a large covered roaster about 45 minutes before the roast was ready to serve. The squash was moist and very tasty with just a bit of butter or the gravy from the roast. You could put a sprinkling of brown sugar on it if you like your squash just a little sweet.

I do not recall Mother having summer squash in her garden, though she always had the big hubbard variety—the last ones to harvest. She split them in two with the axe, removed the seeds and baked them in the oven of the old wood range; this took quite a long time. Then she scooped out the squash, mashed, buttered and seasoned it. This is the perfect squash for taste and texture. It was always on our Thanksgiving dinner table.

October, A Trip To Friends' House

I have a nostalgic longing to visit Mary Ellen and Joe La Palme when October rolls around. They always welcome me warmly into their beautiful home, which is like a second home to me. A sweet sadness envelops me as I walk the colorful wooded hills around Bendon or watch deer feeding under the old apple trees. I am missing loved ones who are not with us anymore, but I am not unhappy.

Mary and Joe are high on my list of beautiful people. They were expecting me, and the delicious aroma of browned beef roast and homemade applesauce greeted me. Joe fixed this squash for dinner.

Wwe can buy squash of many varieties the year-round at our supermarkets; however, they all seem to taste so much better these fall days. We must cook the summer squash before they mature. They include the yellow crook-neck and straight-neck, patty pan and zucchini. These squash varieties and pumpkins are native to America—a gift from the Indians. Here is a delicious recipe from my "Cooking By Touch" cookbook.

Summer Squash Saute

1 lb. summer squash, cut into 1/2-inch slices (do not peel)
3 T. butter
Salt and pepper, to taste

Melt butter in skillet; add squash. Cook over low heat, stirring from time to time, until squash is tender, 5 to 8 minutes. Season with salt and pepper.

This recipe can be varied by combining two varieties of squash; adding sliced green onion to the saute, sprinkling with parsley, chives or basil before serving, and adding peeled, seeded and chopped tomato about 2 minutes before squash is done. Enjoy.

The butternut squash, I believe, is my favorite of all varieties. Just split and remove seeds. Put split-side down on baking sheet and bake at 400 degrees. You also can prick the skin and bake the whole squash until tender, then scoop out the shell, discarding the seeds, mash and season your favorite way. Sometimes I slice and peel butternut squash, cut it in cubes and bake it in a casserole dish with dabs of butter, salt and pepper, baking until tender. I love its nutty flavor.

Apple Pick-Me-Up

Peel 1 medium-large eating apple, cut in small pieces, and put in blender with 1 C. milk and 1 to 2 T. honey. Cover and blend until thick and frothy. Sprinkle with cinnamon or nutmeg. Serve at once. Makes 2 cups.

The old-timers made lots of apple butter, cooking the apples in cider for hours in a big iron kettle with a fire underneath, stirring for hours. My friend, Eula and I were wondering how our people preserved this apple butter before glass jars were available. I am curious about this, thinking it must have been stored in crocks and kept in a cold room or cellar along with the bins of apples and barrels of cider. With their large families, it no doubt did not last long anyway. Last year I bought some delicious apple butter at Nashville House in Brown County, Indiana. They make it there in a large pan in ovens—very good. I like to make this recipe using apple butter.

Our northern state has the perfect climate for apple orchards. At this time in history, 35 states (led by Washington, Michigan and New York) produce about 200 million bushels of apples a year. About one-half are eaten fresh.

The Ancient Celts and Apples

People have loved the apple since the dawn of time. Apples originated south of the Caucasus Mountains and spread all over Europe. Archaeologists have discovered evidence that apples were preserved by drying as far back as the Stone Age. People are still drying them. I also like to think that my ancestors, Britain's ancient Celts, believed in a kingdom of the sun—The Isle of Apples—where there was no old age, sickness or sorrow.

It is no secret that apples are good for us. An average apple has about 85 calories, it provides quick energy with its 12 percent of sugar. It aids digestion. Its pectin supplies fiber and helps to lower cholesterol levels. They contain potassium and vitamins A and C and are 85 percent water.

This morning when I felt the need of some help to get going, I made this pick-me-up and was delighted.

Driving through the multi colored scenes in northern Michigan, I notice the trees in apple orchards with fruit are bending down. This makes me so hungry for a bite of a crisp cold Northern Spy. When I look back in time, I am so thankful that I grew up on a farm with an apple orchard; I could choose any apple I wanted but none compared with the Spy, the last to ripen and picked just before the first killing frost. If I wanted a different flavor, I ate one of those snow apples so red on the outside and so snowy white on the inside; this apple tasted just like apple cider.

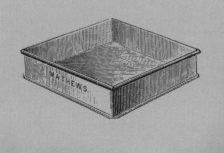

Apple Butter Crispies

Trim crusts from 8 slices of bread. Spread with butter and apple butter. Stack, sandwich-style, in buttered 8-inch square pan. Cut diagonally; combine 1/2 t. cinnamon, 1/2 C. coconut, 1/4 C. sugar and sprinkle over top of bread. Bake in hot oven (400 degrees) for 10 minutes.

We all like apple crisp. Here is one made with honey.

Honey Apple Crisp

4 C. apples, sliced	1/4 C. sugar
1 T. lemon juice	1/2 C. honey
1/2 C. flour	1/4 C. brown sugar
1/4 t. salt	1/4 C. butter
1/4 C. walnuts, if desired	

Spread apples in shallow baking dish, sprinkle sugar, lemon juice and pour honey over all. In bowl, mix flour, brown sugar, salt and work butter in as for biscuits, making a crumbly mixture. Spread crumbs evenly over apples. Bake in 375 degree oven for 30 to 40 minutes. Serve warm with cream or whipped cream.

Apple Spice Muffins

1 pkg. (18-1/2 oz.) spice cake mix
1 can (20 oz) apple pie filling
1/3 C. oil
2/3 C. nuts, chopped
3/4 C. buttermilk
1-1/2 C. Bran cereal
2 eggs

In large mixer bowl, combine all ingredients at low speed just until completely mixed, stirring bottom of bowl once or twice. Batter also can be mixed by hand. Preheat oven to 400. Fill lightly oiled muffin tins 2/3 full with batter. Bake for 25 minutes or until done. Makes 2-1/2 dozen, 2-1/2-inch muffins. If not baking immediately, refrigerate batter up to 10 days.

Friends say that these taste like apple pie in a muffin.

I noticed on our tour this summer that many people were ordering bran muffins for breakfast. Many are making the kind that the batter keeps in the refrigerator a couple of weeks and they bake when they please, or bake them all at once and heat each serving in the microwave. Either method is good. This next recipe is so very delicious you forget about it being good for you, and it is perfect for any meal in the day with all the good-for-us goodies in them.

The topography of the land and the climate of the Leelanau and Old Mission peninsulas are perfect for grapes, and the hills are now lined with beautiful vineyards that are producing wines to compare with the best from California and New York. This last summer on our vacation tour we visited the wine country of the Finger Lakes area in New York, where I picked up some recipes for creative cooking with wines. Now I definitely will visit our wineries this fall when they are picking the grapes. I must know how it is all done!

Grapes—Sun-Kissed Flavor of Fall

Our Michigan grapes render that tantalizing sun-kissed taste of fall that lingers with us this fruitful time of the year. Our shiny, red, gold and pale green apples are the colors of autumn itself, yet one can almost taste the winey fragrance of ripening grapes.

I just looked up the origin of the word "fruit." The Latin word from which fruit is derived is "fructus," meaning use and enjoyment of the produce and income, also the word "frui," meaning to enjoy and delight in. So we are to enjoy our fruits of the earth.

The settlers of Michigan brought their grape vines with them. Many came from New York State where they had cultivated them for years. The most popular were the Concords. Some of the homesteads still have those vines, and we are making jelly again this year.

These vines seem to live forever. I know of one that is at least 75 years old. It has survived through years of drought, cold, heat and neglect. One year we had to wade through tall grass and thick undergrowth to find them, but the grapes were there, sweet and delicious.

My niece and nephew, Mary Ellen and Joe, have restored the old vines by trimming them properly and propping them up, and they produce sweet Concord grapes. Mary Ellen will save some for me.

Grapes of all kinds are definitely for eating fresh, so have them available to munch on and to add to any salad or dessert you are making. The red or green grapes add a tasty and colorful touch to coleslaw or cottage cheese. Serve any variety with cheese for the perfect dessert.

It's jelly-making time and I always advise to use the directions on the package of pectin when making jams and jellies. Following their directions makes for foolproof preserves. However, I am going to give you my old-time recipe for grape jam. This always has been successful through the years for me and brings out the true flavor of the grapes. Be sure the grapes are ripe.

Grape Jam

Wash bunches of purple grapes and pick from the stem. Measure grapes and add to each heaping cupful or (1-1/2 C.), 1 C. sugar. Place both the sugar and grapes in a preserving kettle and heat slowly until the juice starts. Mash and cook for 20 minutes, stirring to avoid burning. Press through a sieve while hot and pour into sterilized glasses and seal. This jam is easier to handle if made in small quantities.

*H*ere are a couple of recipes from the Taylor Wine Company of Hammondsport, N.Y. This is just the kind of casserole to pop in the oven these crisp fall days – a meal in a dish, without a crust.

Zucchini Quiche

3 lbs zucchini
1-1/2 lb. Italian sausage (bulk)
1/2 C. onion, chopped
1/2 C. green pepper, chopped
1 C. Parmesan cheese, grated
1 C. bread crumbs
2 T. parsley, chopped
1/2 t. salt
6 eggs, separated
1/4 C. red wine

Cut ends from squash; boil whole for 10 minutes. Cool and cut into small chunks. Place in colander, drain well. Saute sausage until lightly browned; add onion and green pepper; cook slightly. Remove from heat; combine squash, cheese, crumbs, parsley and salt. Beat together egg yolks and wine; combine with squash and sausage mixture. Beat egg whites until stiff, fold into squash mixture. Pour into buttered 9 x 13-inch pan. Bake at 325 degrees for 45 minutes until set.

Sherried Tomato Soup

1 medium onion, chopped (1/2 C.)
3 T. butter or margarine
1 t. salt
1 can (32 oz.) tomato juice
1/2 C. dry sherry
1 T. honey

1 medium carrot, coarsely shredded (1/2 C.)
1/4 C. flour
Dash of nutmeg
2 C. beef broth
1 T. parsley, snipped

In saucepan cook onion and carrot in butter or margarine until tender but not brown. Stir in flour, salt and nutmeg. Add tomato juice and beef broth. Cook and stir until slightly thickened and bubbly. Add sherry, parsley and honey and simmer until vegetables are tender, about 5 to 10 minutes. Makes 6 servings.

Scary Stories On Nutcracker Night

There is a mystery in the air these fall days and early evenings. One has a mixed feeling of disbelief and awe in observing the changing colors and early darkening nights.

Our ancestors spent more time out of doors. They watched the changes in the seasons and had strange ideas about autumn, when the skies darkened early and they prepared for the long winter ahead. The awesome falling of the leaves and the end of growing for all green things told them that all life did end and they were afraid. They believed in spirits and they believed that fire would frighten them away so it was the time for bonfires.

These ancient rites became a time also to celebrate their harvests and they had their "Nutcracker Night" when they gathered around the fire retelling old scary stories. Special cakes and buns were prepared. Apples always were popular through the years, and they cracked their nuts. In Roman times they had their festival of Ponpana, their goddess of the orchard, in late October.

We know that Halloween always has inspired tricks. In our country serious pranks were played until it became a real problem. I can remember when people's outhouses were tipped over and farm equipment was moved to impossible places such as a neighbor's roof, and windows were coated with wax that had to be scraped off.

Now I am happy to say that the scary part of Halloween is just from the ghosts and goblins that come trick-or-treating. Our children are not afraid of the mysterious things. They watch Kermit the Frog and make-believe monsters all of the time. They love to dress up and pretend. Although we still feel that this is a mysterious time of the year, we understand why the early Christian leaders decided to make these rites into "Allhallows eve" to honor all of the Saints.

I have a wonderful recipe for the children of all ages from my friend Wealtha. It makes 100 cookies and has three of the cereals that kids love in them. They are getting good nutrition in these goodies and they will never be aware of it.

The poet, Keats, described this time of the year as a "Season of mists and mellow fruitfulness." Our harvest is bountiful even after our dry hot summer and we should make the most of it as our appetites are sharpened with the cool air. The old-timers made Brunswick stew. Here is a modernized method for making it. What a delicious dish to take from the oven Halloween or any fall evening. Our forebears would no doubt add a squirrel or rabbit to the stew if they had been lucky hunting.

One Hundred Cookies

Mix together:

1 C. sugar	1 C. brown sugar
1 C. margarine, softened	1 C. vegetable oil
1 egg, beaten	1 C. quick oats
1 t. vanilla	

Then add:
1 C. rice crisp cereal
1 C. cocoa-crisp cereal

Sift together:

3-1/2 C. sifted flour	1 t. baking soda
1 t. cream of tartar	3/4 t. salt

Mix well; drop by teaspoon on ungreased baking sheet and bake at 350 degrees 7 to 10 minutes.

Brunswick Stew

3 slices bacon	3 lbs. chicken pieces

Corn from the cobs of 3 large ears—or use the frozen kind.
2 C. fresh or frozen lima beans
3 large ripe tomatoes, skinned and cut up

2 t. salt	1 t. sugar

2 C. chicken stock—or use the canned kind
pepper to taste

Cut bacon into small pieces and brown in large skillet. Remove bacon and brown chicken pieces in fat. Place chicken and all other ingredients with bacon on top into a large casserole dish. Cover and bake at 325 degrees for 1 hour. Serve with corn bread or muffins.

Old English Wassail

3 cans (12 oz. each) ale
3/4 to 1 C. sugar
10 thin strips lemon peel
3 whole cloves
3 whole allspice
1-1/2 C. dry sherry
1 small cinnamon stick
1 small whole nutmeg, cracked (optional)
Small baked apples or lemon slices (optional)

Pour 1 can ale into heat-resistant glass punch bowl; stir in sugar, lemon peel and spices. Heat, uncovered, in microwave oven on High until simmering, 3-4 minutes. Stir in sherry and remaining ale. Heat, uncovered, in microwave on High, 10 minutes. Stir wassail; remove spices and peel. Float small baked apples or lemon slices in wassail, if desired. Serve in heat-resistant punch cups. Makes 1-1/2 quarts.

Thoughtful 'Treats'

Last year a special person brought me a long stemmed red rose on Trick-or-Treat night. What a nice gesture it was and I have remembered it often. So I believe that Halloween can be a time to do things with friends of all ages.

Halloween is a joyous time for the kids and the very young, a time to celebrate the unusual when the skies darken early on autumn evenings—the leaves are gone from the trees, revealing strange shapes. I can picture in my mind the old-timers cracking nuts in front of their fireplaces and telling scary stories. So why not plan a party for some friends. We oldies would like to celebrate, too.

How about an Old English Wassail made in the microwave for a start?

Juan's Bread Bowl

1 round loaf of bread
1 C. Parmesan cheese

2 C. chopped onion
2 C. mayonnaise

Cut circle in top of loaf; scoop out insides, saving chunks for dipping. Brown onions in saucepan; remove from heat. Add mayonnaise and Parmesan cheese; pour into bread shell. Broil until heated, watching closely so as not to burn. Dip chunks of bread into delicious mixture; enjoy. The bread bowl can be frozen. Note: you can also add crab meat to the cheese mixture.

With the wassail you could serve this luscious and tasty bread bowl. My friend, Juan Acosta, made this recently for us when we visited his family.

Then you might want to have some of these meatballs made in the microwave, then reheat in a crock pot or chafing dish.

Sweet and Sour Meat Balls

1 lb. ground beef
1 T. finely chopped onion
1T. finely chopped parsley
1/2 C. soft bread crumbs
1 egg, slightly beaten

1 t. salt
1/8 t. allspice
1/8 t. cloves
1/4 t. garlic salt
2 T. milk

1 C. pineapple juice
2 T. brown sugar
1 T. lemon juice

1 T. cornstarch

Combine beef, onion, parsley, bread crumbs, egg, milk, salt, garlic salt, allspice and cloves; form into 1-inch balls. Place 8 balls in circle on paper plates lined with double thickness of paper towels; cover with waxed paper. Cook in microwave on High, 1-1/2 minutes, repeating until all are cooked. Combine pineapple juice, brown sugar and cornstarch in 2-cup glass measuring cup. Cook uncovered, in microwave on High, 2 minutes, until thickened, stirring once. Stir in lemon juice. Serve with meatballs. For conventional oven: bake meatballs on cookie sheet in 400-degree oven until browned. You can pick up the meatballs with a toothpick and dip into the sauce—very good. They also are good served with noodles.

Sweet and Sour Venison Meatballs

1-1/2 lb. ground venison
2 C. soft bread crumbs
1/2 lb. ground pork sausage
1/2 C. finely chopped onions
1 can Eagle Brand sweetened condensed milk

1/2 t. pepper
1-1/2 t. salt
2 eggs, beaten
1-1/2 T. prepared mustard
4 to 5 T. vegetable oil

2 bottles (12 oz each) chili sauce
3 to 4 T. Worcestershire sauce
1/2 of a 5 oz. jar cream-style horseradish
1/2 to 3/4 C. water

In a medium bowl combine venison, onions, eggs, mustard, salt, sausage, pepper and 1/2 can of the sweetened condensed milk. Mix well. Stir in bread crumbs. Roll into 1" meatballs (meatballs might be soft).

In large skillet, brown meatballs in vegetable oil over medium heat. Remove from skillet and set aside. Heat chili sauce, Worcestershire sauce and water in skillet; slowly stir in remaining sweetened milk. Add horseradish. You may prefer less than 1/2 of the 5-oz. jar of horseradish. Add meatballs and heat thoroughly, but do not boil. Serve over rice. Serves 8 to 10.

*W*e picture autumn with pumpkins growing in corn fields, like the Indians raised them. They had their venison stews and corn cakes, and I think this is a good time to give you a recipe from Mary Forton. She has been on television a few times for "Michigan Outdoors" and loves to cook using wild game. Here is her own recipe.

Pumpkins, Squash—Gift from Indians

Pumpkins and squash—our gift from the Indians. Sometimes I wonder how people lived before these foods were discovered. It is impossible to imagine a fall dinner without them, as well as cranberries, another gift from the Indians.

The Indians were skilled hunters and fishermen, and the tribes' movements were always connected with food. Whole tribes went to harvest the wild rice all the way to Wisconsin in their birch bark canoes. In winter they were in the woods living on wild game and stored vegetables, and I understand they spent time on the beaches in summer eating seafood. They knew what was good!

Squash is available year round in many varieties, though the hard-skin kind like butternut, buttercup and hubbard squashes are best in the fall. Recently my friend, Anne Jenkins, and I had a squash-tasting party. We heard about the many kinds of spices for pumpkin and squash, so we baked butternut squash by cutting it in half and baked it cut-side down in a pan with about 1 inch of water added. It was tender after about one half hour in a 375-degree oven.

We each took half, divided it in little mounds on our plates and tried the following spices: ginger, cinnamon, cloves, mustard seed, sweet basil and nutmeg. Anne preferred the basil, and I especially liked a little mustard seed and a tiny bit of ginger. We both wanted just a little bit of honey to sweeten the squash. Of course we buttered it and seasoned it with salt to taste before we started our real tasting.

Microwave Squash

Prick holes in a good-sized butternut squash and cook it in the microwave on high for 12 minutes, or until fork-tender, turning it over once. When cool enough to handle, split it, remove the seeds and peel, then mash it up good. Salt and pepper to taste, add a little butter, about 1 T. will do, and 1 T. of brown sugar. Mix it well and put it back in the microwave to reheat a little. We loved it.

My niece, Nellie Childs, always has a very productive garden. She recently served a couple of her "Sugar Dumpling Squash" by fixing two of them the same way as the above butternut squash. "Sugar Dumpling" squash was new to me; it is about the size of a large grapefruit and a beautiful cream color with some stripes of dark green. It also tasted delicious.

I prepared a butternut squash in a different way today, which was very easy to do.

Now is the time to decorate our homes with those little pumpkins and partly husked fancy small ears of Indian corn; a copper bowl with these fall things on the dinner table will brighten the day.

We do not need to wait for a holiday to make this delicious pumpkin cake. Recently my grandson, Joe, asked me if I ever needed a recipe. What a question! His girlfriend's mother made these pumpkin squares, so he asked for the recipe and brought just one piece for me to sample. He said that the rest were going back to Michigan State with him.

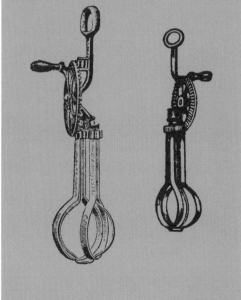

Joey's Pumpkin Squares

4 eggs
1-2/3 C. sugar
1 can (16 oz.) pumpkin
1 C. cooking oil
2 t. baking powder
2 t. cinnamon
1 t. salt
1 t. baking soda
2 C. flour

Beat everything together in a mixing bowl. Spread in a 15 x 10 x 1-inch pan, slightly greased. Bake at 350 for 30 minutes. When cool, frost with this:
1 stick margarine (1/2 C.), softened
1 box (16 oz.) confectioners' sugar
8 oz. cream cheese
1 t. vanilla

Mix all ingredients together until smooth.

I now know why Joey gave me just one piece. It was delicious.

Yule Cake Made When Stoves Set Up

Recently I was fascinated by a picture on the wall in the doctor's office. It looked like a Norman Rockwell painting of a couple taking down the old wood or coal stove.

Soot was everywhere. They were covered with it and I could see the frustration on their faces as they tried to match up the stovepipes with the stove. A tender wave of nostalgia spread over me as I recalled Mother and Dad taking down the stove in the front room every spring, then setting it back up in the fall.

I can see now the beautiful hard-coal stove in the living room. To a small girl it was very big and tall with a ledge on the back for a tea kettle—the old-time humidifier. Coal was fed into the stove from the top; I can see Papa lifting his scuttle of hard coal and pouring it into the top of the stove every night. Then in the morning he used a poker to clean out the grates. The beautiful red coals glowed through the door, which was made of many small sections of isinglass, a preparation of mica in thin, transparent sheets that could stand the heat.

I realize now that even as a young child, I was thrilled with the beautiful fire reflecting into the darkening room before the evening lamps were lit. We never know what memories our children will take with them as they grow up.

At a very young age we learned the difference between the anthracite (hard) coal and bituminous (soft) coal and knew their titles. Later, we had a soft-coal stove that burned wood, as hard coal was not always available and Papa wanted to use his own wood.

About the same time the stoves were setup for the winter, Mama made her Christmas cake; like our fruit cakes it needed to ripen before Christmas. This year I will make the following cake for the holidays.

London Raisin Marmalade Cake

1 C. raisins	2 T. grated lemon peel
2 T. rum	1/2 C. honey
1/2 C. margarine or butter, soft	
2 eggs	
1 C. sweet orange marmalade	
2 C. flour	1 t. ginger
1 t. baking soda	1/2 t. nutmeg
1/2 t. salt	

In small bowl, soak raisins and peel in the rum; set aside. In mixer bowl cream butter. Beat in honey, then marmalade until well blended. Beat in eggs one at a time. Sift flour, ginger, soda, nutmeg and salt; stir in. Add raisin mixture, mixing just to blend. Turn batter into a 9-inch tube pan, greased and dusted with flour. Bake at 350 for 50 to 60 minutes until golden and wooden pick inserted in center comes out clean. Cool in pan 10 minutes; invert onto rack. Warm additional marmalade over low heat to melt; brush over warm cake. Decorate as desired with additional raisins, candied fruit and peels.

Courtesy of California Raisin Advisory Board

Be sure to decorate with some Christmas candies if you have youngsters; that is what I remember most about Mama's cake.

Pumpkin Pie Filling

2 eggs
3/4 C. sugar or 1/2 C. honey
1/2 t. salt   1/4 t. ginger
1 t. cinnamon   1-1/2 C. milk
1 heaping cup cooked pumpkin, or 1 can
(No. 303) pumpkin

Beat eggs and sugar or honey; add other ingredients. Put in pastry lined pie pan. Bake in 450-degree oven 10 minutes; reduce heat to 300 and continue baking, 45 minutes, until knife inserted in center comes out clean.

I came across this recipe for pumpkin pie and I made it to be sure that it had the old-time flavor, and it did. Add a few more spices if your family expects them.

Pie Crust

For 2-crust pie:
2-1/4 C. flour
1 C. vegetable shortening
Tiny pinch of salt
Ice water

My family still likes my old-fashioned pie crust better than any other kind.

Cut shortening into flour and salt mixture, using 2 knives or pastry blender, until lumps are size of small peas. Add ice water very gradually until dough sticks together somewhat; then using hands, lightly form into ball. Divide in half; flatten out into balls and roll between sheets of waxed paper, using just a very little flour on waxed paper. Remove top layer of paper; invert pie pan on top of crust, turning upside down. Carefully remove bottom layer of paper. Do the same for top crust by removing the top paper, then place it on top of pie and remove the other layer of paper.

A good cook once told me to use the water as if it were gold, using as little as possible when making a pie.

If you want to sneak something new into the Thanksgiving dinner, you usually can do it with the salad. Broccoli is a modern favorite vegetable and I think they will welcome it in this salad.

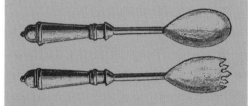

Thanksgiving

My Mother and Father were married on Thanksgiving Day, 1900, so through the years there was a double reason for a celebration. I recall their silver anniversary when the aunts, uncles and cousins congregated to our farm, bringing their casseroles, pies, cakes and silver spoons for a happy Thanksgiving dinner when I was about 12 years old.

Broccoli Salad

1 medium-size bunch of broccoli
4 hard-boiled eggs, chopped
1 small onion, chopped
3/4 C. green olives, halved
1/4 C. pickle relish
2 T. lemon juice
2/3 C. mayonnaise

Trim tough parts off broccoli; soak in salt water. Drain well; cut into bite-size pieces. Add eggs, onion, olives and pickle relish; mix well lemon juice and mayonnaise, pouring over ingredients. Mix well; let set overnight. Makes 8 nice crunchy servings.

Sausage and Corn Stuffing

1 lb. bulk sausage
3 medium-sized onions, chopped (1-1/2 C.)
8 C. day-old bread cubes
1 T. dried parsley flakes
1-1/2 t. poultry seasoning
1 t. salt
1/4 t. pepper
1 can (17 oz.) cream-style corn

Cook sausage in large skillet, stirring to break up, until browned; remove from skillet. Pour off all but 1/4 C. sausage fat.

Add vegetable oil, if necessary to make 1/4 C.; cook onion in fat until soft. Combine bread cubes, parsley, poultry seasoning, salt and pepper in large bowl; add onion mixture, sausage and corn, tossing until well combined.

After stuffing the turkey I always have dressing left over. Put in a casserole and bake it the last 45 minutes to one hour while the turkey is still roasting.

Nearly everything on mother's Thanksgiving table was produced on the farm and she made her own bread and rolls—even her butter. However, there was one luxury that she always bought at the store; it was fresh cranberries. There was always a pretty bowl of cooked cranberries in the center of the table. For me, Thanksgiving dinner would not be complete without that bowl of cranberries. Happy Thanksgiving!

Thanksgiving is the time to cook all the old family favorites. I have found that we cannot deviate from them—experimenting with a new recipe is not the thing to do here. Sometimes I even serve both squash and sweet potatoes to satisfy family members. Through the years I have tried to fancy-up pumpkin pies, but it just does not work—they want just old-fashioned, plain pumpkin pie—no fancy fixings, just some whipped cream to top it for some. They also expect apple pie.

The turkeys at our supermarket are easy to prepare and are tender. Follow the directions on the package. The turkey is done when the little button pops up. My family would be disappointed if I did not make their sausage and corn dressing.

My friend, Joyce, who once gave me so many delicious recipes said that she always added a few more nutmeats than the recipe called for which makes "good—better." This next recipe does not tell how many nuts to use; however, more would be better.

I have long been curious about chestnuts, mainly because of Longfellow's poem.

"Under the spreading
        chestnut tree,
The village smithy stands,
The Smith, a mighty man is he
With large and sinewy hands,
The muscles of his brawny arms
Are strong as iron bands."

We memorized this poem in school, though I do not remember what a chestnut tree looked like. By the time I had heard about them they were almost extinct. My Audubon books tell me that in 1904 it was discovered that a blight was killing the chestnut trees in New

Hungarian Pound Cake

1 lb. margarine, whipped	6 eggs
1 lb. confectioners' sugar	1 t. vanilla
3 C. flour, unsifted	cinnamon
granulated sugar	nuts, chopped

Reserve enough margarine to grease sides and bottom of Bundt or angel food cake pan. Sprinkle cinnamon and sugar on sides, nuts in bottom. Cream margarine and sugar; add eggs one at a time, beating well after each addition. Add flour and vanilla. Mix well and bake at 350 for 1-1/4 hours. (May be frozen, even refrozen. Great with ice cream and sauces.)

The Nutting Season

In many recipes we see the words "Nuts optional" and one can be sure that the results will be better flavor and texture if they are used.

This is the nutting season. They are about to fall off the trees in our area. Some of my friends put them in their driveways and drive over them to remove the outer husks. By holiday time they are ready to be cracked and to pick out the nut meats. What a chore it used to be. All kinds of nutmeats are on our grocer's shelves and they are all commercially picked and shelled for us. How lucky can we get?

Black and white walnuts or butternuts grow in our woods, along the highways in our area; hickory trees grow in the southern part of Michigan. We have beechnuts that are fun to gather; although it takes a lot of labor to shell a small amount, the flavor is worth the trouble. Chestnut trees are making a comeback after being destroyed some years ago by a fungus. Michigan chestnuts are now being sent to other states for replanting. The thin-shelled English walnuts that were imported by our ancestors are so very popular because they are easy to crack. They have been grown commercially since Roman times. Our pecans grow naturally in the Mississippi Valley from Iowa southward. Texas is the largest producer of pecans, producing up to 95,000,000 pounds a year.

Nuts are probably one of the most ancient of all foods. They were used extensively by our native Americans. There are many references to them in the Bible. Appetizers in Old Testament times were salted almonds or other nuts and cheese eaten with pieces of bread dipped in wine.

York's zoological gardens. This fungus disease spread fast through the next few years to cover the whole area where the trees grew— from Maine to Mississippi. "From the few dying trees of 1904, in New York City, the disease has gone on to slaughter the equivalent of 9 million acres of the American chestnuts."

Now, we have the good news that chestnut trees are being grown successfully in our northern areas again. And, I can hardly wait for a taste of those nuts. I am told that they have a sweeter flavor than the European chestnuts. We can put so many of our everyday foods in the gourmet class by adding a few nutmeats to the recipe. We put them in our cakes, cookies, muffins, pies, salads of all kinds and even in our vegetable dishes. Add some pecans with a little honey to your baked squash or sweet potatoes. You will be glad you put peanuts or water chestnuts in your next broccoli salad; also, anything made with apples, cooked or raw, is enhanced with nutmeats.

Your kids will love these easy-to-make cookies.

Then for the gals at tea time, honor them with these luscious goodies.

Graham Cracker Cookies

1 C. light brown sugar
1 C. butter or margarine
1 C. chopped nutmeats
25 graham crackers

Place graham crackers on cookie sheet. Boil sugar and butter rapidly together 1 minute; add nuts to mixture; pour over top of graham crackers. Bake at 350 for 7 minutes.

Turn off oven; let remain in oven 3 more minutes. Remove from oven; slice into small squares.

Tea Time Tasties

1 pkg. (3 oz.) cream cheese
1/2 C. margarine
1 C. sifted flour   1 egg
3/4 C. brown sugar   1 T. soft margarine
1 t. vanilla   Dash of salt
2/3 C. coarsely-broken pecans

Cheese Pastry:

Let cream cheese and 1/2 C. margarine soften to room temperature; blend. Stir in flour; chill 1 hour. Shape into 24 1-inch balls. Place in tiny ungreased 1-3/4-inch muffin cups, pressing dough on bottom and sides of cups.

Pecan Filling:

Beat egg, sugar, 1 T. margarine, vanilla and salt together just until smooth. Divide half the pecans among the pastry-lined cups; spoon egg mixture into cups. Top with pecans. Bake at 325 for 25 minutes; until set. Remove from pans.

Pea and Peanut Salad

1/3 C. mayonnaise
1/4 t. dill weed
2 T. sour cream
1/4 t. dry mustard
1/2 t. sugar
1/2 t. vinegar
Dash of salt
1 C. Spanish peanuts
1 can (16 oz.) peas, drained

Blend all ingredients, folding in peas and peanuts last. Chill. Makes 4 servings.

The above recipes were taken from Thelma Bentley's 1972 cookbook compiled and edited by United Methodist Women, St. Paul's United Methodist Church, Rochester, Michigan. Thanks, Thelma.

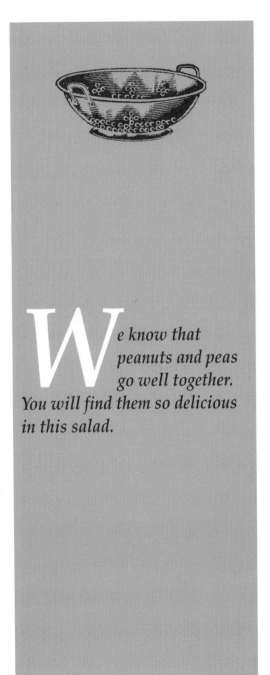

We know that peanuts and peas go well together. You will find them so delicious in this salad.

Winter

This is one of those days when I feel sorry for those people who feel sorry for us Northerners when winter arrives.

We are now having our first snow that really covers the ground. The birds came to the feeder in flocks this morning; they always know when a storm is coming. I am lingering with my morning coffee, watching the big flakes hurriedly settle down and I am excited all over again to see our seasons change before my eyes.

The old-timers would be out getting the wood stacked in cords, and I am sure that they wondered if they would have enough for the long winter months ahead. If not, they could cut more wood and haul it home on the bobsleds or go to town for a load of coal.

Everyone in our North Country has access to a four-wheel-drive vehicle with a plow on the front and our roads are always open except in the middle of a storm.

I hope you enjoy our modern and old-time recipes for winter—a good time of year to cook. Winter appetites call for lots of good down-home food.

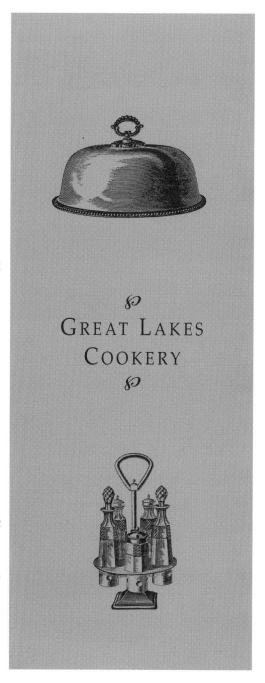

ᗮ
GREAT LAKES
COOKERY
ᗮ

Snow Day Nostalgia

How quiet it was the day of our first real winter storm. Our electricity was off; no TV or radio and no sound from the dishwasher, vacuum cleaner, humidifier or refrigerator. Even my typewriter was of no use. I lit a couple of candles and played a game of solitaire. This put me into a quiet, happy nostalgic mood, a time to think about how our grandparents lived. I thought about how our people lived before central heating. They did not have to worry about the heat turning off because it needed electricity to run; they just needed more trips to the woodpile.

Furnaces in basements were rare at the time I was growing up on the farm. The stoves were above ground and our basement was filled with potatoes, apples, canned fruit and big crocks of pork or pickles in brine. We had a large, full-size basement with a cement floor. We called it the cellar. Many houses had what was called a Michigan basement. It had a shelf all around, and a small basement was dug inside of it. The Michigan basement usually had a dirt floor. Fruits and vegetables were kept at a good cold temperature all winter without freezing.

Grandmother's home also had a pantry, usually a narrow, walk-in closet-type room with shelves all around the walls and places to hang pots and pans. The old pantries were very handy; everything was within reach. I am happy to see that many people who are renovating old homes are keeping the pantry, and I notice that walk-in pantries are being built in new homes.

We are not canning everything the way that Mother did. However, I like to buy canned vegetables and fruit in the fall when our stores have their harvest sales. If I had a pantry I would really take advantage of those sales. We like to have soup on these cold winter days when we are sitting out a storm.

What delicious dishes can be prepared if we have canned tomatoes in our cupboard. Of course we always have beans, rice and pasta on our shelves, and wonderful goodies can be made with oatmeal and corn meal. Try these for a surprise supper with ham or bacon and maple syrup.

For years I looked for a good recipe for corn meal griddle cakes or batter cakes, and I found this one from an old Rumford Baking Powder cookbook on household economy. I do not know the date that it was published but it was before the electric mixer was in use.

Delicate Cornmeal Griddle Cakes

1/4 C. corn meal	1/2 t. salt
1/2 C. cold water	
1-1/2 C. boiling water	
1 level T. shortening	
3/4 C. cold milk	
2 egg yolks	1 level C. flour
4 level t. baking powder	
2 egg whites beaten very light	

Stir the cornmeal with the salt and cold water, then stir into the water boiling directly over the fire. Continue to stir and cook until the mixture thickens; cover and let cook over boiling water 20 minutes, stirring occasionally. Add the shortening, the cold milk, the egg yolks, the flour sifted again with the baking powder and lastly the egg whites. Scoop at once by tablespoon onto a hot griddle. This recipe makes between 30 and 40 small cakes.

Venison Spinach Roll

Meat mixture:

1-1/2 lbs. ground venison
1/4 C. catsup
1/4 C. milk
2 eggs, slightly beaten
2 slices soft bread, cut into small pieces
1/2 t. salt
1/4 t. pepper (white)
1/2 t. oregano
1/2 t. garlic powder
1/2 t. onion powder

Filling:

1 pkg. (10 oz.) frozen leaf spinach
1 t. salt
1 pkg. (3 oz.) smoked pressed sliced ham

Topping:

3 slices of Mozzarella cheese cut diagonally into halves

Those who went hunting will no doubt have some ground venison in the freezer. Here is Mary Forton's recipe for Venison Spinach Roll. The listing of ingredients and quantities is in the order that they are used.

Thaw frozen spinach by rinsing with hot running water to separate and remove ice. Drain; set aside. Mix meat mixture ingredients.

On a piece of foil pat meat mixture into shape about 10 x 12 inches. Arrange spinach evenly on top of meat. Sprinkle the 1 t. salt on the spinach. Arrange ham in layers on top of the spinach. Carefully roll up meat, beginning at narrow end and using the foil to lift the meat. Press edges and end of roll to seal. Place on an ungreased 11 x 7-inch baking dish. Pour 1/2 C. water around the meat. Bake uncovered in 350 degree oven for 1 hour and 15 minutes. When roll is done, overlap cheese slices on top of roll. Bake just until cheese begins to melt, about 5 minutes. The center of the meat may be slightly pink because of the ham.

Grandma always had to have dessert and her well-stocked pantry always had a jug of molasses in it so she could mix up this easy cake at the last minute. She made this when the hens were not laying and she was short on sugar. Old-time cooks from New England, the South and Michigan have sent me this recipe. Here is Marguerite McNiel's recipe.

Sugar Molasses Cake

Pour 1 C. boiling water over 1 C. molasses and 1/2 C. shortening.
In another bowl, mix with wire whip:

2 C. flour	1 t. soda
1 t. cinnamon	1/2 t. ginger

Mix with the first ingredients and bake at 350 degrees 30 to 40 minutes. Grease and flour the baking pan.

Grandmother would have topped this cake with whipped cream, though we probably will have a whipped topping in the freezer or refrigerator.

Christmas Memories— Preparing For Holidays

Christmas is the time to make memories for our families. Many of us have beautiful memories stored up from Christmases past. My first ones are of our front room, the red carpet with rose designs, the old organ so tall that I thought it went to the ceiling. I remember thinking that it was the place where babies came from. Heaven was up there somewhere.

I can still see the glow from the hard-coal burner and our stockings hanging from a broomstick mounted on the back of two dining room chairs. I do not remember having a Christmas tree at that time. However, I recall going to Grandma's house where she had a tree. I suppose I really do not remember speaking my piece at Grandma's where I stood on a chair and recited:

> I'm Papa's little Darling
> I'm only three years old
> Santa Claus will come to my house
> 'Cause I'm just as good as gold.

I was told about it through the years.

I would like to share with you some ideas from an editorial written by my niece, Bonnie, for her church newsletter. She wrote "Some of my fond memories are of studying quilts made by my grandmother and recognizing the little pieces of material. This past Christmas my mother delighted my little daughter and five other granddaughters with 'recycled' dolls complete with handmade wardrobes from just such scraps of material. My Heather is enthralled with her beautiful doll that belonged to me when I was her age."

*C*hristmas trees were introduced to America by German settlers and mercenaries in the early 1700s, but were not generally accepted until more than 100 years later. Then they became popular in the towns and in cabins on the frontier as well.

People once saved scraps of cloth, yarn and cotton for dolls. I remember one year when Mother bought new heads for our old dolls. You could send to Sears Roebuck for doll heads for 10 cents or a quarter then. Of course she made new clothes for those dolls. I wonder now when she found the time.

Bonnie's sister, Norma, expressed her thoughts about those dolls in a poem.

Love and Recycling

Recycling isn't merely making
    something new from old.
It's turning memories from yesterday
    into gifts worth more than gold.
For I can never take my daughters
    back in time;
But as they see the clothes I wore
    now on their dolls so fair
In clothes out of material
    put together with such care,
We have an added bond you see
    that brings us closer still,
For my dear mother made them all
    Out of scraps and love and will.

Now let's get down to basics with some recipes for the holiday season, from my mail box. How about this punch for one of your first parties.

Jingle Bell Punch

2 qts. cranberry juice (chilled)
1 can (6 oz.) frozen lemonade, thawed
1/2 C. maraschino cherry juice
6 bottles (7 oz.) of Sprite or other lemon-lime beverage, chilled

Combine all ingredients except Sprite. At serving time pour over ice in punch bowl. Add Sprite. Servings may be garnished with slices of lemon, orange or a maraschino cherry on a stick. It's real good plain. 40 servings.

Cheese Spread

Break into chunks 1 lb. Velveeta cheese, room temperature. Add 1/2 C. mayonnaise, 1/4 C. vinegar, 1/3 C. sugar. Beat mixture and add 1/4 C. mayonnaise and 1 jar pimientos, chopped, and the juice. Mix well.

That's all there is to it, though sometimes she separates the cheese before she starts and adds pimientos to some, then in another bowl mixes some of the cheese with black or regular olives.

Any way you fix it this makes a good sandwich spread or dip. Be as creative as you like at this point.

Peanut Butter Bars

1 C. butter or margarine
1 C. peanut butter
1 (1 lb.) box powdered sugar
7 Hershey bars

Melt butter; add peanut butter and sugar. Mix well by hand. Spread in buttered cookie sheet. Press out with hands. Break up Hershey bars on top of peanut butter. Put under the oven broiler until chocolate melts (no longer than 2 minutes). Spread evenly. Put in freezer for 15 minutes or until chocolate is hard. Cut into squares.

Chinese New Year's Cookies

1 pkg. (6 oz.) semi-sweet chocolate
1 pkg. (6 oz.) butterscotch bits
1 can (3 oz.) Chinese noodles
1 can (7-1/2 oz.) salted peanuts

Melt chocolate and butterscotch bits in double boiler over hot water. Add noodles and nuts. Drop on waxed paper by teaspoons. Chill. Makes 48 cookies. From Dorothy Liscum, Boyne City.

My friend, Wealtha, makes this cheese spread; she says that it freezes well, so she makes a double batch and has it handy to entertain at any time.

My granddaughter, Diana, makes these cookies or candies. Kids of every age will love them.

You might not want to wait until New Year's for these.

Holiday Finale

Appetizer to Dessert

Christmas dinner is the grand finale of the holiday celebrations. The tree has been decorated, gifts given and received, the community and school programs are over, and we are ready to top it all off with our traditional and favorite foods. The turkey is roasted to perfection, the snowy mashed potatoes are piled high and the cranberries, favorite salads and desserts are ready.

First we will have an appetizer—as if it were necessary. I am going to serve a seafood cocktail. I have made this one through the years and served it as a first course. However this year I will serve it mixed together in a bowl as a dip or spread with crackers and chips with a holiday punch. This has quite a long list of ingredients but it is worth all the effort.

Seafood Cocktail

1 can crabmeat, rinsed in cold water, drained
1 can shrimp, remove vein if any, blanch in hot water, drain, chill.
When ready to serve, mix with this Cocktail Sauce (recipe follows)

Cocktail Sauce

1/2 C. mayonnaise
1/4 t. salt
Pepper & 1/8 t. paprika
1/2 C. chili sauce
1/8 C. India relish or pickles, finely chopped
1 hard-cooked egg, finely chopped
1 t. chives or green onion, minced
1 T. pimiento, minced
1 T. celery, minced
1 t. prepared mustard
Dash of Tabasco

Mix together and chill. For more than six you will need to double this recipe.

Sausage Stuffing

8 oz. savory sage or original roll sausage
1/2 C. margarine or butter
1-1/2 C. onion, chopped
1 C. celery, chopped
1-1/2 C. water
1 C. instant chicken bouillon
1 t. poultry seasoning
4 C. dried bread crumbs
1/4 t. pepper
7 oz. corn bread stuffing mix or 8" square
pan of cornbread, crumbled
1 C. toasted pecans, broken
1 egg, beaten

In large skillet crumble and brown sausage; remove from skillet; drain. In same skillet melt margarine; add onion and celery; cook until tender. In large bowl combine all ingredients with sausage; mix well. Stuff turkey loosely immediately before roasting.

Roast turkey as directed on wrapper. Spoon any remaining stuffing into greased baking dish. Bake at 325 degrees 45 to 50 minutes if cooking separately. Refrigerate leftovers. Makes enough to stuff a 12-lb. turkey.

*J*ust the spicy aroma of this stuffing will make everyone hungry.

Joyce's Cherry Chiffon Cake

2-1/4 C. flour, sifted
1-1/2 C. sugar
3 t. baking powder
1 t. salt
1/2 C. cooking oil
5 medium egg yolks, unbeaten
1/4 C. maraschino cherry juice
1/2 C. cold water
1 t. vanilla
1 C. egg whites (7-8 eggs)
1/2 t. cream of tartar

Sift flour, sugar, baking powder and salt together. Make well in center and add oil, egg yolks, cherry juice, water and vanilla. Beat with spoon until smooth. Whip egg whites and cream of tartar until very stiff; do not underbeat. Pour egg yolk mixture gradually over whites and fold gently; do not stir. Gently add 1/2 C. thinly sliced, well-drained maraschino cherries. Bake in ungreased 10-inch tube pan at 325 for 55 minutes; then at 350 for 10-15 minutes; invert to cool. Sift powdered sugar over cake after it has cooled if you wish. It makes a beautiful dessert.

This meal calls for a light yet colorful dessert and I would like to suggest this beautiful cake.

Auld Lang Syne

Auld Lang Syne becomes more meaningful and special to us as the years hasten by. I remember when I wondered why everyone sang it on New Year's Eve. Now I know: we sing it in memory of parties in the past and for the friends and loved ones who are not with us. It is a happy-sad song linking the past with the future, and we love to sing it.

There are many different kinds of New Year's parties and celebrations across our land. However, the kinds I remember the best are those small intimate parties with very special friends and loved ones. This year I am sending my greetings from my daughter's home in California. Happy New Year!

Coconut Thumbprint Cookies

1 C. butter or margarine
1/4 t. salt
1 C. confectioners' sugar, sifted
1 t. almond extract, optional
1-3/4 C. flour, unsifted
1 C. coconut, flaked
3/4 C. almonds, ground or finely chopped and blanched, optional
Jelly, jam, marmalade or preserves for topping

Cream butter and salt; gradually beat in sugar. Blend in almond extract; add flour a little at a time, mixing well after each addition. Stir in coconut and almonds. Chill dough. When ready to make, roll small amount into small balls. Place on ungreased baking sheets. Bake at 325 degrees 8 minutes; remove from oven. Make depression in center of each with thumb or measuring spoon; return to oven. Bake 12-15 minutes until lightly browned. Cool on sheets; fill each cookie with 1 t. topping. Sprinkle with more coconut, if desired. Store in loosely covered jar. Makes 4 dozen cookies.

Families have their own special foods and games for New Year's Eve. We need tidbits to munch on before the clock strikes 12, when we drink to the new year. My daughter's family always has a tray of cheeses, crackers and deviled eggs. We usually have fruitcake left from Christmas and a tray of these coconut cookies will go beautifully with your eggnog. They also are fun to make.

On New Year's Eve all of the food should be prepared ahead of time so that everyone can enjoy the party. We want to serve nonalcoholic beverages for those who want them. Another thing to remember is that our eggnog does not have to be spiked. Here is a delicious cider.

Here is one more delicious snack from our microwave cooking class.

Spiced Cider

2 qts. apple juice	4 cinnamon sticks,
16 allspice, whole	whole
2 T. brown sugar	16 cloves, whole
4 oranges, sliced	2 lemons, sliced

This can be made in large saucepan on stove or in microwave. In 3-quart bowl combine all ingredients. Microwave on high 15 minutes, uncovered. Stir; let stand one hour; remove spices. Heat to serve warm.

Snack Time Kabobs

1 can (15 oz.) luncheon meat
1 T. brown sugar
1 can (1 lb.) pineapple chunks
2 T. soy sauce
1 T. vinegar
Toothpicks

Cut meat into 60 cubes. Drain pineapple chunks; cut in half. Place one on each toothpick; arrange in singer layer in dish. Combine sauce ingredients; spoon over kabobs; marinate 1 hour. Transfer to platter. Cook 30 at a time for 2 minutes on high. Turn dish one-half turn; spoon sauce over kabobs; cook 1-3/4 minutes. Makes 60 kabobs.

Ham

1 3-lb. canned ham
1/2 C. brown sugar
2 t. mustard, dry
1/4 C. orange marmalade
A few whole cloves

This is another microwave recipe. It also can be made in your oven. Just give it a little more time to heat and glaze.

Place ham in dish; microwave on high 5 minutes. Remove from oven; score top. Place cloves into top of ham. Combine remaining ingredients; spread over ham. Microwave 10 minutes; baste several times. Let stand 10 minutes. Cool for sandwiches.

Coffee should be served before the night is over and your friends will appreciate some food with it.

My husband's favorite after-midnight snack was Braunschweiger and Swiss cheese on rye slices with a little horseradish sauce. Let everyone make his own sandwich and have some thin slices of ham from the deli for those who prefer it.

Here is an easy way to fix ham if you want to do it yourself. Very good either hot or cold.

Pigs were Linked with Ancient Gods

On a 2,500-year-old vase at the Louvre in Paris is a painting of a pig being offered in a ritual slaughter to a god.

Swine, both domestic and wild, were linked with deities in ancient cultures around the world and were sacrificed to many gods. Hence, there were taboos against eating pork.

From my old National Geographics, I find that swine first appeared on earth some 36 million years ago, which makes them somewhat older than man. They never were native to the Western Hemisphere, although there was a close relative—the peccary. The great-grandfather of our modern pigs was the European wild boar.

Columbus supposedly left pigs on Haiti when he landed there. From that original stock, they were spread throughout the West Indies, many returning to their wild state. After 400 years there are still descendants of these wild hogs on islands off the coast of Georgia and Florida, and some in the state of Florida. (On a cold wet foggy morning last winter in central Florida a friend, to my surprise, pointed out a wild boar to me. I was glad we were riding in the car!)

Swine were no doubt on all colonial ships coming to America later, and pork became the main meat for our ancestors all through the colonial and pioneer periods. Here are a couple of "Economical Recipes" from an old cookbook.

Sauteed Salt Pork

Cut pork in 1/4-inch thin slices, cover with boiling water and cook five minutes. Drain, arrange in frying pan and cook slowly for five minutes, then more rapidly until crisp and brown on both sides.

Cottage Pie

1 C. chopped meat
1 C. hot water or gravy
2 C. mashed potatoes
1/2 t. salt
1/2 C. hot milk
1 T. butter
Few grains celery salt
1/2 t. pepper

Put meat in casserole; add salt and pepper to taste, and the hot water. Mix the mashed potatoes with the remaining ingredients and spread on top of meat; bake in hot oven until potato mixture is brown.

Not too many years ago, the fatter the hog the better for butchering, because our forefathers needed the fat for lard and other uses. Now with our vegetable shortenings, the high-cholesterol lard is no longer needed, and many of us thought we should cut down on our favorite pork products.

This is what Grandma would serve with pancakes and applesauce for breakfast or for an unexpected guest when she was out of bread. We can now purchase fresh side pork at our supermarkets, and I would like to prepare this recipe with it.

Then there is cottage pie, which can be made with leftover roast pork or beef.

Kraut-Pork Pinwheel

The pork industry has done a great deal to overcome this. They are raising slimmed-down hogs, and most of our meat now has a lot less cholesterol. They do not fatten the hogs and they butcher them when they are 6 to 7 months old. So enjoy the good pork available. Some experts say that good lean pork has no more cholesterol than breast of chicken.

When I told my friend Maxine Schlink that I was writing about pork, she immediately invited me to share a meal of spare ribs and sauerkraut, of which we are both very fond. Great-Grandpa and Grandma made barrel-sized crocks full of kraut every fall. What a wonderful way to preserve their cabbage.

My friend, Rosalyn Chapel, gave me this recipe from her fabulous collection. It is another terrific way to serve those two go-togethers, pork and sauerkraut.

1 lb. ground pork
1/2 C. dry bread crumbs
1 beaten egg
1 t. salt
Dash of pepper
1/2 t. Worcestershire sauce
1-lb. can (2 C.) drained sauerkraut
1/4 C. chopped onion
5 slices bacon

Combine pork, bread crumbs, egg, salt, pepper and Worcestershire sauce. Mix thoroughly. On wax paper pat meat into 10 x 7-inch rectangle.

Combine sauerkraut and onion; spread evenly over meat. Starting at the narrow side, roll up jelly-roll fashion. Place loaf in shallow baking dish. Arrange bacon slices across top. Bake in 350 oven about 45 minutes or until golden brown and bacon is crisp. Serve with mashed potatoes. Mashed potatoes are a must with spare ribs and sauerkraut. Maxine puts her kraut on top of the potatoes just like gravy.

Mmmmmmmm-good! And don't forget the applesauce!

Little Dumplings

1 egg
3 T. flour
Pinch of salt
1 t. vegetable oil

Mix the egg with flour, salt and oil. Meanwhile heat soup. Spoon the mixture into boiling soup, using 1/4 t. measuring spoon for size. Cook in soup 2 to 3 minutes.

Chili Mac

1 lb. ground beef
1 C. chopped onion
2 medium cloves garlic, minced
1 can (14-1/2 oz.) ready-to-serve beef broth
2 cans (10-1/2 oz.) each condensed tomato
    soup
2 cans (15-1/2 oz.) each kidney beans,
    undrained
3 C. cooked elbow macaroni
3 T. chili powder
2 T. vinegar

In heavy large pan, brown beef and cook onion with garlic until tender; stir. Add remaining ingredients. Cook over low heat 30 minutes. Stir occasionally. Makes 6 servings. From Creative Food Center, Campbell Soup Co.

Suddenly, I am inspired to make a pot of soup, some home made bread or just some little dumplings for a stew already made. Then I notice that the sun is shining.

This recipe for little dumplings comes from Marguerite McNiel, so good in any soup or stew.

Our grandmothers spent many hours making their own broths and stocks for soup. We have neither the time for this nor the cuts of meat that they had, such as sheep's head, neck of mutton or beef marrow bones. We can make delicious soups from canned broth, however. They are tasty and nutritious. Follow recipes on cans or add your own touches. The following is made with canned broth.

Overcoming Cabin Fever

It is easy to let a consuming type of lethargy take over these days when the snow is blowing and the mercury goes almost out of sight. We call it cabin fever and wonder how we are going to overcome it.

Then I can begin to understand why the poet Robert Frost stopped his horse along a country road on a snowy evening. As I look out my window toward a small woodlot, I think of how easy it would be to linger and watch the woods fill up with snow. Then I repeat his words:

The woods are lovely, dark and deep,

But I have promises to keep,

And miles to go before I sleep

And miles to go before I sleep.

Last winter my friend Lillian introduced me to some of those dry soup mixes, and I was impressed. We like to go out to lunch for our main meal, then after an afternoon of sightseeing or shopping we had soup for supper. She soon had soup simmering on the stove, and the aroma perked up our appetites as we nibbled on cheese and crackers with a little glass of wine. After a bowl of those tasty soups we were content with just a salad or dessert.

Since then I have been doing a little experimenting with the wonderful variety of soup mixtures on the market. One of my favorites is Leek Soup and Recipe Mix. After following the directions on the box for the initial preparation you can add goodies to taste. here are some ways to use leek soup:

- Add a few cooked peas
- Top bowl of soup with grated cheese and zap in microwave just to melt
- Use the soup for a sauce for creamed chicken or fricassee
- Cook some finely diced potatoes in the soup for a potato soup flavor
- If you add pieces of cooked chicken, you can believe you are eating authentic Scottish cock-a-leekie soup.

Fruit Salad

4 apples, unpared, in chunks
1/2 C. celery, chopped
1/2 C. dates, chopped
1/2 C. pineapple tidbits, drained
    (save juice)
1/2 C. walnuts, chopped
1/2 C. salad dressing

    Combine fruits. Mix salad dressing with 2 T. of the pineapple juice. Add to fruit mixture. Add nuts and serve. Serves 6.

Cucumber and Radish Salad

1-1/2 t. sugar
1 t. salt
Dash of pepper
1 T. lemon juice
1/2 C. thinly sliced cucumbers
Radish roses or slices
Parsley for trim

    Combine the first four ingredients. Stir in cucumbers. Chill. Serve on lettuce leaves as an appetizer or salad. Garnish with radish slices and parsley.

Salads are a must with soups. Vegetable tossed salad and slaws go with the creamed soups and fruit with the vegetable soups and stews.

A cottage cheese and fruit salad will complement that Chili Mac dinner. Spice up your pineapple or peach and cheese salad with slices of kiwi fruit for an extra touch. Or try this slightly different combination of fruits.

I have a friend who loves radishes; I think he will enjoy this salad. It is a good contrast to creamed soups or a nice relish for any dinner. This recipe is for one or two; increase as needed.

*J*ust the aroma of these beans baking will make one almost forget the cold north wind. Newlywed Kim Courtright Wright makes this recipe. She already has started a tradition; we will expect her to bring these beans to our potlucks in the future.

Kim's Baked Beans

1 can kidney beans (drained)
1 can butter beans (drained)
1 can pork and beans
1 C. chopped onion
1 C. catsup
1 C. brown sugar
1/2 lb. cooked bacon (crumbled)

Mix all these ingredients. Bake 350 degrees until thickness desired. I do not believe it matters too much about the size of the cans, as long as they are uniform in size.

*D*orothy Leslie, who winters in the sunny South, sent me this recipe. It could be called a sweet potato pie; it makes one almost think it is a dessert it is so good. She said it was served when they were invited to dinner at the home of a native Southern gal who said that she was going to cook real Southern food.

Sweet Potato Casserole

3 C. cooked sweet potatoes
1 C. sugar
1/2 C. evaporated milk
3 eggs
1/2 stick margarine, melted
1 t. vanilla

Put all ingredients in a bowl and mix with electric mixer. Pour into greased 2-quart oven dish. Cover with topping and bake 30 to 45 minutes at 350 degrees. (The time will vary depending on whether it is a deep or flat pan.) If a knife inserted in the center comes out clean, it is baked enough.

Topping:
1 C. brown sugar
1/4 C. flour
1/2 stick margarine, softened
Dash cinnamon
As many chopped pecans as you wish

Mix all together with a pastry blender or fork and sprinkle over the casserole.

Beans and Corn Bread

When I hear the country music song "Cornbread, Beans and Sweet Potato Pie," it puts me in the mood to do some cooking. My kitchen is the most cheerful place in the house on these gray winter days when meteorologist Bill Spencer reports that an "Alberta Clipper" is on the way and we will have lots more snow.

I have a few snow-day recipes to share. Of course, beans and corn bread come first. I suppose that I am in a rut, as I am impelled to dig out John Greenleaf Whittier's "Snow Bound" to read; I do this yearly. Perhaps it is because it recalls memories of snow days on the farm, and I revel in the description of "No cloud above, no earth below; a universe of sky and snow!"

Valentine's Day – A Needed Holiday

"Roses are red
Violets are blue
Sugar is sweet
And so are you"

This was one of the first poems we learned and we printed it on our homemade Valentines even before we went to school. Then later we had the Valentine box in the school, which was a large cardboard box covered with pretty wallpaper with a slot on the top to put the Valentines in. Then we wondered about how many Valentines we would receive when the box was opened. The girl or boy with the most Valentines would be considered the most popular one in the school. Then later, it did not matter how many we received so long as that very special one came, especially if it had "Isle of View" written on it.

We all have this need for these expressions of love in our lives and it must have always been so, because something comparable to Valentine's Day has been celebrated throughout many cultures and countries. It has been a time to give little tokens of our love, and food has long been the way to express our love.

Cranberry Ribbon Pie

1 pkg. (3 oz.) lemon-flavored pudding mix
1/2 C. sugar
2 C. water
1 egg, slightly beaten
3/4 C. cranberry orange sauce
1 pkg. (8 oz.) cream cheese, cut in cubes
1 T. grated orange rind
2 C. thawed non-dairy topping
1 9-inch Graham cracker crumb crust or
regular pie crust, baked

Combine pudding mix, sugar and 1/4 C. water in saucepan; stir in egg and remaining water. Cook, stirring, until mixture comes to full boil. Measure 3/4 C. and blend in cranberry sauce; chill. Add cream cheese to remaining filling, stirring until cheese melts; add rind. Chill 30 minutes or place in freezer for 15 minutes. Fold in whipped topping; pour half of cranberry mixture over cheese filling. Top with remaining cranberry mixture. Freeze 1 hour or chill 3 hours before serving. Garnish with additional whipped topping and orange sections or slices, if desired.

Valentine's Day is an opportunity to have an intimate family dinner, a time to use your best dishes and pretty placemats or tablecloths with a nice centerpiece and candles. One's family needs something like this occasionally in these busy times. You might put together this beautiful pie for dessert.

*C*akes, cookies, fruits and candies always have been Valentine gifts. I imagine that almost every one of us have a few heart-shaped boxes or pretty dishes in the house. Why not fill them with some homemade candies and give to a person to whom you want to show your loving care?

Here are some candy recipes from "Islanders Cook For Company." This book is from the United Methodist Women of St. Andrew By The Sea, Hilton Head Island, S.C.

Jane Manring makes these buckeyes every year for their fall festival. She brought her recipe from the Buckeye State and it's easy to do, though you might want to have some help when dipping them, which is a little time-consuming.

Candy Buckeyes

1 lb. butter or margarine, melted
2 lbs. smooth peanut butter
3 lbs. confectioners' sugar
2 pkg. (6 oz.) each semi-sweet chocolate bits
1/4 lb. (1 stick) paraffin

Mix first 3 ingredients together thoroughly in large mixing bowl; form into small balls. Place in refrigerator to chill 2 hours or overnight. Melt chocolate bits and paraffin in double boiler until smooth; keep warm while dipping. Place toothpick in candy ball; dip in chocolate. Don't cover completely. Place on wax paper; lift out toothpick, smoothing top. Continue process. Makes 150 pieces.

Peanut Butter Balls

1 C. peanut butter
1 C. powdered milk
1/2 C. honey
1/2 C. wheat germ

Mix peanut butter, powdered milk and honey together; roll into small balls. Roll in wheat germ. Keeps best in refrigerator.

Rice Crispy Balls

1/2 C. honey
1/2 C. powdered milk
1/2 C. peanut butter
1/2 t. vanilla
4 C. Rice Krispies

Heat honey; remove from heat. Add powdered milk, peanut butter and vanilla; mix thoroughly. Pour over cereal; form into small balls. A yummy nutritious snack.

These next two recipes are very easy to do and really are good for children of all ages.

Let the children mix this up for snacks to share with their friends.

Soup Rejoices the Stomach

In Edna Baney Brown's book "Mabel's Kitchen" she tells how her grandmother, Rachel, raised eight children alone on her farm in Lapeer County after the death of her husband. This is the way she made her bean soup.

Bean Soup

"It took large quantities of food to feed this growing family. Rachel would place a large iron 3-legged pot in a hole of the kitchen cookstove. Then she would place in it dry beans and water, fat salt pork, onions, carrots, celery and rutabagas to make a tasty soup. Parboiling was to make the beans less gassy, hopefully."

She raised all of the above vegetables in the muckland on her back forty near Imlay City.

Parmentier Soup

"Slice 4 potatoes and 3 young onions. Cook the onions in 4 tablespoons of butter for 2 minutes; then stir in the potatoes, add 1-1/2 quarts of water, cook 2 hours, put through a sieve, add a little cream mixed with an egg yolk, salt and Rawleigh's black pepper."

Winter is soup time. A bowl of hot soup is welcome after removing ice and snow from the car or shoveling the driveway. An old cookbook writer says, "soup rejoices the stomach and disposes it to receive and digest food." I believe that! There are so many ways to make potato soup and every cook thinks that his or her ways are the best.

Here is a recipe from a "Rawleigh" book published in 1917. If you are wondering about the title, Monsieur Parmentier introduced the potato into France and was honored by King Louis XVII for doing so. A statue in his honor was erected in the center of Paris with potato plants growing around it.

*T*he winter solstice is past and the days are longer; however, we need to remind ourselves that spring finally will come. A good way to do this is to prepare these next pre-taste of spring soups.

Cream of Asparagus Soup

1 can (14-1/2 oz.) asparagus pieces
1 medium onion, chopped
1/4 C. flour
1/4 C. butter or margarine
1/2 t. salt
1/4 t. nutmeg
milk

Drain asparagus, reserving liquid. Cook onion in butter until soft; stir in flour and seasonings. Cook, stirring, until pasty. Add milk to reserved asparagus liquid to make one quart; add to flour mixture. Cook, stirring, until slightly thickened. Whirl 3/4 of asparagus in blender; add to milk mixture. Heat through. Garnish with croutons, shredded cheese or toasted sunflower seeds. Makes 6 servings.

Amy's Cheese Broccoli Soup

1/4 C. chopped onion
1 T. margarine
1 pkg. (10 oz.) frozen broccoli, chopped and cooked according to directions, or cook fresh broccoli until tender in the same proportion
Dash of pepper
2 C. milk
2 chicken bouillon cubes
1 T. cornstarch
1 pkg. (8 oz.) cream cheese

Cook onion in margarine in 2-quart saucepan until soft; add 1-1/2 C. milk and bouillon cubes. Bring to boil. Thicken cornstarch in one-half C. of milk; add to mixture, cooking until thickened. Add broccoli; cook over low heat, add cream cheese, stirring until hot.

Broccoli soup is a very popular one with people of all ages. This next one is a real yummy one—another tried-and-true recipe from Amy Courtney.

Savory Beef Casserole

Now, here is a heartwarming stew to serve your family on one of these cold winter nights. It's a meal in a dish. A dessert—like apple crisp or peach cobbler could be baking at the same time for a real old-fashioned delicious supper.

1-1/2 lbs. beef stew meat
Seasoned flour with salt, pepper and other seasonings
3 T. shortening
2 medium onions, finely chopped
1-3/4 C. water
1 can condensed tomato soup
1 small bay leaf
1 stalk celery, sliced
4 carrots, cubed
3 medium potatoes, cubed
1 C. peas*
Salt and pepper, to taste

Cut meat into 1-inch cubes; dredge with seasoned flour. Brown in hot fat; transfer to 3-quart casserole. Lightly brown onion in hot fat; add to meat. Blend water with tomato soup; pour over meat. Add crushed bay leaf and celery. Bake, covered, in 325 degree oven 1-1/2 hours, until meat is tender. Cook carrots, potatoes and peas until almost tender; drain. Add to meat; season to taste. Bake 30 minutes. Makes 8 servings.

*Canned or frozen peas do not need to be cooked before using.

Cherries

We must serve cherries in February to honor George Washington. We are reminded of the story about him cutting down his father's cherry tree with his little hatchet. Of course he told his father the truth about it because he could not tell a lie. The Reverend Mason Lock Weems wrote the story. It just might not be exactly true as the Rev. Weems liked to exaggerate and he most always had to have a moral to his stories; however, it has had some credence through the years. So, cherries in February? Of course!

Cherries are beautiful. "Cherries are magic: They glow," says Deni Hooper who really knows her cherries. I wonder sometimes about the poet who wrote, "Life is a bowl of cherries." He was most likely in love at the time. I believe that cherry trees always thrive in the most beautiful regions of the world. They love the cooling breezes off Lake Michigan and they seem to be extra fond of northern Michigan hillsides.

I just returned from an extended trip to California and I was thrilled with the grandeur of the mountains, deserts and the Pacific Ocean. Yet I did not see anything any more beautiful than our own cherry orchards in blossom time, harvest, or in the winter when the white snow contrasts with the deep blue sky. No matter where I go I think that I will always be just a little bit homesick for our Great Lakes region and that means cherries.

Our hotel and country-inn chefs specialize in cherry recipes and I wonder if we will ever scrape the bottom of the barrel when it comes to cherry recipes.

*T*his next one is new to me: a deep-dish cherry pie with a new way with the crust and a meringue-type cake topping. I made it in a regular 10-inch pie pan.

Deep-Dish Cherry Pie

1 C. flour	1 T. powdered sugar
1/2 C. margarine	1 can cherry pie mix

Sift flour and powdered sugar together; cut in butter. Pat evenly over bottom and sides of 10-inch deep-dish pie pan. Bake in moderate oven 350 degrees for 15 minutes until lightly browned. Spread cherry pie mix over partially-baked crust; top with Meringue Cake Topping.

Topping:

2 egg whites	1 C. sugar
3/4 C. flour	1/2 t. baking powder

3 T. coffee cream or half-and-half
1 t. vanilla
3/4 C. coarsely chopped pecans
1/2 C. flaked coconut

Beat egg whites until very frothy, gradually add sugar a little at a time; beat until stiff peaks form. Sift flour and baking powder together; fold in meringue mixture alternately with cream. Fold in vanilla, nuts and coconut; do not beat. Turn out over top of cherries. If desired, arrange a crown of candied cherries and chopped pecans over meringue. Bake in moderate oven 350 degrees for 30 minutes; do not over-bake. I baked mine 45 minutes to a golden brown and the top was baked too hard. However, it was very tasty and my friends loved it.

Cherry Delight

4 oz. margarine, room temperature
1 C. sugar
1 C. crushed pretzels
1 – 8 oz. pkg. Neufchatel cheese
2 containers (8 oz. each) non-dairy
whipped topping
1 can (21 oz.) cherry pie filling

Mix margarine, sugar, 3/4 C. pretzels together; press into 9 x 13-inch pan. Mix Neufchatel cheese and 1 container non-dairy whipped topping together in large bowl; spread over pretzel layer. Spread cherry pie filling over all; top with remaining container of non-dairy topping. Sprinkle remaining 1/4 cup pretzels on top. Chill in refrigerator 3 hours before serving.

I can always find delicious easy-to-make recipes in my "Cooking by Touch" book. Here is one.

*T*hen there are these recipes from Deni Hooper's "Magic Cherry." Maybe you have some frozen sweet cherries in your freezer. What a delicious dessert they make.

Fresh Sweet Cherries Frozen

They are a real gourmet treat. Beware of eating too many too fast or you will regret it. A few at a time will do well as dessert, snack or garnish. Freeze unpitted with stem if you like for a mid-winter treat. You might dip them in this topping.

Chocolate-Dipped Cherries

8 oz. semi-sweet chocolate

Heat over hot water until partially melted; remove from heat, stirring until melted. When cool to touch, dip cold cherries in chocolate. Place on waxed paper to harden.

Cherry Compote

1 can (21 oz.) red tart cherry pie filling
1 can (15-1/2 oz.) pineapple chunks with syrup
1 C. dried apricots
2-1/2 C. water
3/4 t. cinnamon

Place together undrained in 3-quart casserole; bake at 350 degrees 1-1/2 hours.

*I*f you have Deni's cherry compote in the refrigerator, you will have a delicious colorful dessert on hand. It keeps well but just might not last long when your friends get a sample of this one.

I am happy to see some new cherry products on our market shelves. I like the canned cherry applesauce; it is delicious with a dish of cottage cheese. Black sweet cherry pie filling is another goodie. So let's indulge and brighten up these winter days.

At this time of the year I like to search through my files for recipes with a foretaste of spring—parsnips come first to my mind. Grandmother had to wait for the snow to melt and the ground to thaw enough to dig up parsnips from her garden. How good they tasted!

Groundhog Day—A Hint of Spring

I often wonder how Groundhog Day really started. Everyone living in the northern United States needs a reminder that after six more weeks, at the most, spring is bound to return.

By the first of February we wonder just how long winter will last and we need assurance that there will be long, sunny days ahead. That need for assurance must be as old as time. I suppose that people from different backgrounds have various stories about the questionable arrival of spring. When I was very young, my father told us that on the second day of February the bear came out of his cave to see if spring was there yet. If he saw his shadow he was frightened and went back in for six more weeks of sleep.

Now, it seems that on February second there is always some part of the day when the sun will peep through so that a shadow can be seen and the animals will continue their winter naps.

My Audubon books tell me that "Chuck," "Groundhog," and "Whistle Pig" are common names for the woodchuck. Also, by February second they are most likely hibernating but by the first of April they are all out, searching for mates and food.

Parsnip Patties

To serve: Wash and boil one large parsnip or 2 smaller ones until very tender in salted boiling water. Scrape off skin and mash to a pulp while hot. Add one heaping t. each of butter and flour and 1/2 t. salt. Stir well; add yolk of 1 egg; mold into four little flat cakes. If the mixture sticks, dip hands in cold water, shake off drops and proceed. Dip cakes in powdered cracker crumbs. When cold, fry to delicate brown in hot butter. It will take a teaspoon of butter for each side. Do not cook longer than necessary to brown and heat through or egg will harden and cakes lose their creaminess. Serve these with tender fried ham and stewed tomatoes for a real country supper.

We are now fortunate enough to be able to find parsnips at the supermarket almost any time. Parsnips are best fried. This is the way Grandmother did it from "Catering for Two," published in 1898. They are still delicious and remind me of spring.

I f you do not feel like making the patties, you can still relish the spring-like flavor of parsnips this way from "Catering for Two."

Buttered Parsnips

Boil one large parsnip in salted water until tender; scrape and cut into halves lengthwise. Dredge with flour and pepper; fry to brown in spoonful of butter.

Baked Apricots

2 cans (15 oz.) apricots, lightly drained
Light brown sugar
2 cups Ritz crackers
1 stick butter or margarine, melted

Place layer of canned apricots, sprinkling of light brown sugar and layer of crushed crackers in buttered 9-inch square baking dish. Repeat layers; pour melted butter over top. Bake at 300 degrees for 50 minutes.

H ere is a tasty cheerful dish to add to any early spring meal. Put it into the oven with a meat loaf or serve it with any menu. It is a delicious accompaniment to any meat dish.

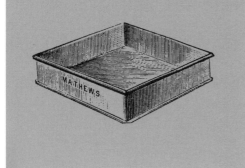

Don's Stir-Fried Veggies

Stir fry shredded cabbage, carrots and leeks in small amount of olive oil to lightly coat pan. If leeks are not available, use green onions, using part of green tops. Use about equal amounts of these vegetables or choose vegetables of your choice. Cook until crisp-tender; season with soy sauce to taste. No salt is needed with the soy sauce.

We can depend on vegetable dishes for color and nutrition these early spring days. Enjoy them fixed this way. It is especially easy if you received a food processor for Christmas.

Special People and Places

I have long had the opinion that the people we cook for are more important than the cooking itself. So, I am dedicating this section to those very special people and to the beautiful places that I have been privileged to visit. I discovered a long time ago that the secret ingredient in any recipe is love.

These recipes are for all seasons, with love.
Bea Smith

Food Roads Well Traveled

Americana cooking has become a delicious potpourri of ethnic foods. My memory tells me that cooking has become more exciting as the years go by. The original foods of the Indians were basics like fish, venison, other wild game and birds, squash, pumpkin, beans, corn and wild fruits. What roads our foods have traveled to get to our tables! How exciting to travel those roads like the one that our potato has traveled—originating in South America then Europe, Ireland and back to the New World.

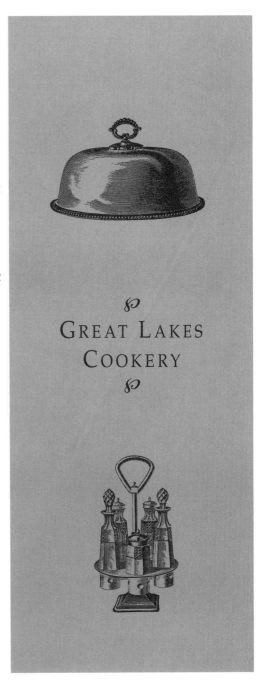

ᔥ
GREAT LAKES
COOKERY
ᔥ

ᔐ GREAT LAKES COOKERY ᔐ

Before the Jamestown or Plymouth colonies were settled, Spanish explorers were learning about the Mexican and Indian foods of the Southwest—their beans, corn and peppers.

Our early English, Dutch and French settlers brought their grains like oats, wheat, barley, seeds and cuttings for fruit trees, beef, pork and cheeses.

Later, other groups brought their Greek cheeses and vegetables, Italian pastas, Hungarian goulash, Swedish smorgasbord, Irish and Scottish scones and oat cakes. We could go on and on down the food trails; there is no end.

Men as well as women have traveled down those food roads—Columbus discovered American foods as well as lands. Thomas Jefferson introduced many French recipes such as ice cream to the American public. He also helped to make the tomato popular. Early hunters and trappers had their own methods of cooking game and fish. Here are some truly American recipes from men who like to cook and to eat.

Baked Fresh Salmon

Thaw the fish if frozen. I used the microwave for this. Put fish sliced 1-inch thick into glass baking dish according to size of fish. Salt and pepper; spread fish with softened butter or butter-flavored margarine. Spread thin layer of dry onions, next a layer of crumbled wafer crackers. Bill says to spread all of these ingredients evenly over fish but do not coat too heavily. Pour milk into dish half way up on fish; bake at 375 degrees until fish flakes and is lightly browned. Bill caught this fish in Lake Michigan near Charlevoix and it was delicious.

Venison Swiss Steak

Bill cuts venison steak into serving-sized pieces, pounds flour into them and fries them in oil until brown. Add salt and pepper, a little chopped onion, 1 can mushroom soup and a can of water. You might need to double the soup and water if you have more meat. Put everything into crock pot, set at low, and let it cook all day. When he gets home from work or hunting, his dinner is fork-tender and ready for him and his friends. I have eaten some of this venison and it is delicious.

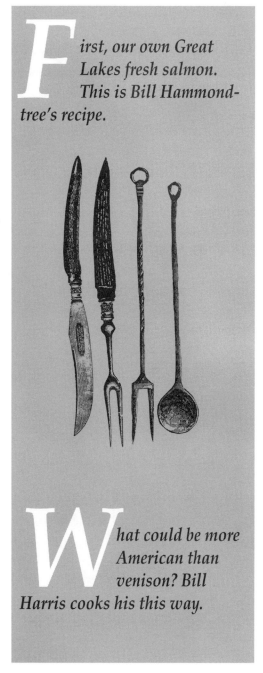

First, our own Great Lakes fresh salmon. This is Bill Hammond-tree's recipe.

What could be more American than venison? Bill Harris cooks his this way.

Men really like their desserts. Bob Sidur of Hilton Head, S.C. discovered this one at his favorite restaurant on the Island and they gave him the recipe. This recipe also has traveled far. His friends in Michigan love Bob's special dessert. My friend, Lillian, makes it often and her granddaughter, Cynthia, gave me the recipe in Marshall last summer. This mousse keeps beautifully in the freezer. Cynthia had some for me to sample—luscious.

Recipe—Both Old and New

We sometimes like a fresh approach or a little surprise in our day-to-day cooking, which makes me wonder—could there be anything new in egg cookery? This next recipe is something new to me, yet it is very old.

I was transported into another time when my daughter and I visited the old-time kitchen in the fort at Mackinaw City.

Bob's Lemon Mousse

3 C. vanilla wafers, crushed
Juice of 6 lemons, no more than 6 oz.
2 C. sugar and a bit more
2 lemon rinds grated
2 cans (12 oz. each) evaporated milk

Put evaporated milk into bowl; freeze 1 hour. Remove; beat milk until stiff; add juice, sugar, rinds and blend well. Put 1-1/2 C. crushed wafers in bottom of large springform pan; pour in mousse and top with remaining 1-1/2 C. wafers. Freeze overnight; store in freezer.

Scots Eggs

6 hard-boiled eggs
1 lb. seasoned bulk pork sausage (I used the old style seasoned with sage)
Flour and cracker crumbs

Boil the eggs, peel and dry. While you are doing this, set the sausage out of the refrigerator. It handles better at room temperature. Cut the eggs in half crosswise and roll in flour, which makes it easier to coat with the sausage. With wet hands coat the eggs with the sausage, making balls. Roll in cracker crumbs.

You can have all of this done ahead of time, and just before serving fry in deep fat, using your deep fat fryer. (I did it by pouring non-cholesterol oil about 1 inch deep into a fry pan and frying them until crisp and brown, turning once.) They were delicious. Thanks, Lucy; we loved them and I will make them often, thinking of you.

I heated a leftover egg in the microwave for my breakfast this morning—very good!

Lucy Hume, from an old pioneer family of the area, has spent many summers in the fort kitchen. She explains how wool was spun for yarn the old way when spinning wheels were not common and she describes everything used in the old kitchen of the 1700s.

Of course the main part of the kitchen was the fireplace. This one had a swinging crane but no side oven. Everything was baked or cooked in heavy iron pots set in front of the fire. Hooks of different lengths were made by the local blacksmith to roast meats at just the right distance from the glowing coals. Lucy had baked a cake the day we were there, a beautiful pound-style cake.

The Scots played an important role in the history of the fort while the English were in control. I was told that the Royal Highland Engineers moved the fort to Mackinac Island. So Lucy gave me this old-time recipe, knowing my Scot's ancestry. I made these eggs and we were delighted.

Here is another oldie that is still always welcome. Grandma made lots of custards when the hens were laying. This is from a booklet put out by the Detroit Creamery in 1917. It also can be made in custard cups.

For those of us who need to cut down on eggs because of high cholesterol level, Egg Beaters can be used for almost everything made with beaten eggs. Egg Beaters, found in the frozen foods section at the supermarket, are good for making pancakes, omelets, scrambled eggs or French toast. Here is a delicious beverage.

Egyptian Caramel Custard

1/2 C. sugar, caramelized
3 eggs
2 C. scalded milk
Few grains salt
Few grains nutmeg
1/2 t. vanilla
1/4 C. sugar

Caramelize (melt) the 1/2 C. sugar over moderate heat, stirring constantly, and pour at once into a tin or aluminum mold, tipping it until the syrup is hardened on the bottom and half way up the side. Then beat the eggs, add the sugar, salt and flavorings, and pour the scalded milk into it. Turn into the lined mold, set this in a pan of hot water and bake in a slow oven. (I would set it for about 300 degrees.) Chill and unmold. The syrup will have colored the lower part of the custard, the remainder having melted to form a sauce.

Citrus Cooler

3 C. orange juice   1/2 C. egg beaters
2 T. honey

In blender, blend orange juice, Egg Beaters and honey about 30 seconds. Serve immediately. Makes 6 servings.

Honey

Honey is as old as time. It is referred to often in the Old Testament. In early Bible times, unleavened bread was eaten with honey, honey was used to sweeten wine that had been diluted with five parts of water for the table beverages. From Proverbs, "Eat honey, for it is good, and the drippings of the honeycomb are sweet to your taste."

Honey Dip

1/2 C. honey
2 t. lemon juice

Measure honey into glass measure; add lemon juice.

Microwave on high 45 to 60 seconds until hot. Serve with chicken.

This reminds me of how good that honeycomb tasted that my father brought home when he did the shopping. Honey eaten from the comb had no comparison with strained honey. I remember how I chewed on that honeycomb until all of the sweetness was gone. I wonder now why things never taste that good anymore. Maybe it is because, in our affluent society, we have so much that we do not take the time to savor the abundant produce that is given to us. So let's enjoy our honey. Make this simple dip the next time you have fried chicken in any form.

Special People and Places

L et us not forget to season our vegetables with honey; it brings out the flavor of:

A nother quote from the Old Testament: "And the house of Israel called the name there-of Manna; and it was like coriander seed, white; and the taste of it was like wafers made with honey." Here is a honey of a tip, when making your favorite bran muffins, line the pans with this:

Honey Glazed Carrots

3 T. butter
1 T. water
8-10 medium carrots, sliced very thin
1 t. + 1 T. honey
Minced parsley, for garnish

Combine butter and water in heavy 8-inch skillet; add carrots. Sprinkle with 1 t. honey; cover tightly. Simmer over low heat, 12 minutes until tender, stirring occasionally.

Drizzle with 1 T. honey; top with minced parsley. Makes 4 to 6 servings.

Bee Hives

1/4 C. brown sugar
1/4 C. shortening
2 T. honey

Cream brown sugar, shortening and honey; line muffin tins. Fill pans one-half full with muffin batter. Bake 15-17 minutes until golden brown. Remove from pans while hot by inverting pan onto rack. I used a 7-ounce Jiffy muffin mix and it was enough for 8 delicious muffins.

Vegetable Pizza

For the pastry:

Roll 2 pkgs. of croissant or crescent rolls from the supermarket dairy section on a cookie sheet or large pizza pan. Bake at 375 degrees until golden brown; this takes about 10 minutes.

For the filling:

Cream together 1 pkg. (8 oz.) cream cheese and 8 oz. mayonnaise. Mix in 1 pkg. ranch-style salad dressing (dry). Spread on the cooled crust.

Then top with a mixture of raw vegetables like small heads of broccoli, sliced green onions, coarsely chopped green peppers and radish slices. Top with shredded Cheddar cheese. No, you do not heat this pizza, you eat it at room temperature or cold. Serve it in small squares or wedges as hors d'oeuvres at your next party; your friends will love it.

If you have the vegetables prepared ahead of time, you can put this together in a very few minutes when friends drop in.

Pizzas

When we ponder on the reason why a certain food is a favorite we discover that texture, flavor and aroma are the real reasons why we love it. A good pizza has it all. It is a favorite of all ages and it is so much fun to eat.

This popular recipe has been making the rounds in our area. My granddaughter, Barb, gave it to me. She said that her friend, Bobbie-Jo, gave it to her and she did not want to take the credit for it as she received it from another friend. A good recipe like this one travels fast. My daughter, Shirley, says that this is a "you-can't-stop-eating pizza."

"Pizza pie" as we first called it seemed to have been Italy's best kept secret until after WWII, then its popularity grew by leaps and bounds; and no wonder, the aroma of fresh-baked bread alone would make everyone hunger for it. Mother used to fry bread dough on a griddle once in a while and how I loved it. Nothing whets the appetite like that fresh-baked bread fragrance. Then add the Italian sauces, cheese and other condiments and you have it made.

I like to do things the easy way. You might want to have extras of these next pizza muffins—so great for snacks or to tote to the office for lunch. Keep in refrigerator or freezer until ready to heat. I picked up this recipe at a microwave cooking class.

Pepperoni Pizza Muffins

For one serving:
1 English muffin, split
1 tablespoon pizza sauce
2 T. pasteurized processed cheese spread
6 slices pepperoni
2 ripe olives, sliced

Place muffin halves, cut side up on a paper towel. Spread with cheese spread. Top with pizza sauce, pepperoni and olives. Microwave (high) uncovered 30 to 45 seconds or until cheese is melted and bubbly. Tips: Other favorite pizza toppings can be used. If you like more cheese, just add a slice of Mozzarella before adding pepperoni. Picante sauce can be used in place of pizza sauce. So experiment and enjoy.

Pizza Rolls

Use either stove or microwave methods.
1 lb. ground beef
1/4 C. finely chopped onion
1 clove garlic, pressed or finely chopped
1/2 C. thick tomato sauce
1/2 t. basil or oregano
1/2 t. salt
1/4 t. pepper
2 Italian rolls, about 6″ long each
3/4 C. shredded Mozzarella cheese

Microwave method: Combine beef, onion, and garlic in a 1 qt. glass baking dish. Cover, microwave at high 7-1/2 to 9 minutes or until beef begins to brown, stirring twice. Drain off fat. Stir in tomato sauce, oregano, salt and pepper. Split rolls in half lengthwise and arrange in an oblong baking dish. Spoon on beef mixture and top with cheese. Microwave uncovered at low for 11 to 12 minutes or until cheese is melted and sandwiches are hot.

Stove method: Combine beef, onion and garlic in saucepan; cook on stove top at medium heat until beef starts to brown, stirring occasionally. Drain off fat. Stir in tomato sauce, oregano, salt and pepper. Heat thoroughly. Split rolls and arrange on baking sheet, spoon on beef mixture and top with cheese. Bake at 375 degrees until cheese is melted and rolls are hot.

*I*f you want to serve four people in a hurry you can make these pizza rolls.

Boat Galley Recipes

I had qualms. I was not sure that I could be a good sailor when we planned a weekend on Don's sailboat. We were to sail from Marina Del Rey to Long Beach, California.

We went to a fast-food place and stocked up on sandwiches and salads for the trip and sailed out about noon on Saturday. I was transported immediately into another world and was very relieved to find that we were always within sight of land. We saw seals resting on the buoys and tanks, porpoises, and on the way home, we sighted a whale.

I could not believe the size of the Long Beach Harbor. I learned that there are marinas where people can register their boats and stay for the night. We arrived at ours just before dark. These marinas have everything for the traveler: places to shower and dress, and within walking distance to restaurants and other shopping places. We had a delicious dinner at a Rusty Pelican, then back to the boat.

I had misgivings about sleeping. I was to sleep in the little galley where a bed was made up on top of the stove. There was a bed in the bow for Don and Gloria. The gentle motion of the boat and the sound of the water lapping its side put me to sleep almost immediately. I was up with the sun the next morning and Don put the stove to use making our breakfast—the best breakfast I ever had: sausages, eggs, hash browns, English muffins and good hot coffee. This meal was to last us until we arrived back at Marina Del Rey. We sailed around the "Queen Mary" and Howard Hughes' "Spruce Goose" and arrived home just before dark. My diary for that day reads, "Feb. 27, 1982. Will relive this trip over and over again in my pleasant memories." This is the kind of memories that boat owners all over are making for their families.

Galley-Style Meat Loaf

1-1/2 lbs. ground beef
1 t. Worcestershire sauce
1-1/2 C. dry bread crumbs
Salt and pepper, to taste
1 lb. ground pork
1/2 C. diced carrots
1/4 C. milk
1/4 C. chopped onion
2 eggs, beaten
1/4 C. celery, diced

Combine all ingredients; mix well. Place in 9 x 5-inch greased baking loaf pan. Bake in 350-degree oven, 1-1/2 hours or until done.

*N*ow Don is rebuilding his small kitchen at home to be exactly like a real ship's galley. A sailor from way back, Don knows that everything has to have its own solid place and the need to use the minimum amount of utensils. So our recipes must be the kind to use just as few dishes as possible. Many times when weather is rough, the recipe must be very simple with few ingredients; however, at other times the cook can go all out preparing gourmet foods. In most ships' galleys anything that can be cooked in an apartment kitchen can be prepared.

Put some potatoes to bake in the oven with this meatloaf and you will have a stick-to-the-ribs meal for hungry sailors. I toasted fresh bread lightly to make the bread crumbs. My family really likes this meatloaf.

This is the kind of soup Don would make either at home or on his boat.

You might not be making fancy desserts; however, salads are always in demand. Here is an old recipe from a "Wilkin Whisky Book." This is just the way my mother made it.

Tuna Broccoli Soup

1 can (7 oz.) tuna
1 pkg (10 oz.) frozen, chopped broccoli
3 T. butter or margarine

2 T. flour	1 t. onion salt
Dash of pepper	Dash of nutmeg

1 qt. milk
1/3 C. liquid from broccoli

Drain tuna; break into large pieces. Cook broccoli as directed on package; drain, saving liquid. Melt butter; blend in flour and seasonings. Add milk gradually; cook until thick and smooth, stirring constantly. Add broccoli, liquid and tuna; heat. Serves 6.

Mother's Coleslaw

1 head cabbage	1 C. sugar
1 t dry mustard	1 t. salt
Dash of pepper	2 eggs
1 C. top milk	1 C. vinegar

Cut cabbage in quarters; soak in cold water until crisp. Drain; shred fine. Mix sugar, mustard, salt and pepper. Add eggs; mix well. Add milk; add vinegar slowly. Cook over low heat, constantly stirring, until thickened; chill. Pour over cabbage. Mrs. Wilkins states that "this recipe has been in our family for 80 years, passing from generation to generation."

Old-Time Catfish With a Modern Image

There is a new kid on the block—catfish! Old-time catfish has a new image. All around our country people have discovered the farm-raised variety available at their supermarkets. The texture is firm and the taste is mildly sweet. It is good for us; it is low in saturated fats, high in protein, low in calories and sodium and a good vitamin and mineral source. Farm-raised catfish are not scavengers; they are fed a pellet mixture of soybeans, corn, wheat, vitamins and minerals.

My friend, Lillian, took her granddaughter and her husband to a lovely dinner at a restaurant. Gorham ordered catfish. Lillian was astounded; "why not order something nice," she said. "Wait until you taste it," he told her and Lillian soon discovered that it was the best item on the menu.

Now she tells everyone about the delicious catfish. She insisted that I order it when we went for lunch.

Larry Elder of Charlotte, N.C. won a $2000 prize in a catfish cooking contest held in Nashville. His recipe is simple to make yet elegant and so tasty.

My son-in-law, Don, insists that catfish should be dipped in cornmeal and fried in hot lard like his mother fixed it when he caught them, as a boy in Florida. He likes to fix any fish fillets this way in the microwave.

Farm-Raised Catfish Lorenzo

6 (4-5 oz.) farm-raised catfish fillets, fresh or frozen
1 jar (1/2 C. or 4 oz.) honey mustard
1 C. cashew nuts, roasted and finely chopped
3 T. parsley, chopped, optional
1 lemon, sliced, optional

If frozen, thaw fish according to package instructions. Preheat oven to 350 degrees. Place fillets on well-greased baking sheet in single layer; generously brush with honey mustard; sprinkle with chopped nuts. Bake 10-12 minutes until catfish flakes easily. Garnish with lemon slices and parsley if desired. Serves 6.

Poached Fish

12 oz. fish fillets, fresh or frozen, thawed
1/2 C. dry white wine
1/4 t. salt
1/8 t. pepper

Place fillets in square 8 x 8 baking dish; pour wine over fillets. Sprinkle with salt and pepper; cover with plastic wrap. Microwave on medium until fish flakes easily in center with fork, 10-15 minutes. Makes 3 or 4 servings.

Cable Car Tuna Casserole

6 oz. egg noodles, cooked and drained
1/2 t. thyme
1/4 t. salt
1 can (10 oz.) cream of celery soup
1/2 C. milk
2 cans (7 oz. ea.) solid white meat tuna,
    drained and flaked
1 C. celery, coarsely chopped
1/2 C. green pepper, coarsely chopped
1/3 C. water chestnuts, sliced
1/3 C. scallions, with some green tops
1/2 C. mayonnaise
3/4 C. sharp cheddar cheese, grated
1/4 C. almonds, chopped and toasted

Preheat oven to 425 degrees. Combine noodles, thyme and salt in 2-quart casserole; set aside. Mix soup and milk together in saucepan; heat, stirring constantly, until smooth. Add tuna, celery, green pepper, water chestnuts, scallions, mayonnaise and all but two T. of the cheese. Heat, stir until cheese melts. Add cheese sauce to casserole; mix thoroughly. Sprinkle with remaining cheese and almonds. Bake 20 minutes until bubbly and lightly browned.

What would we do without a good tuna casserole? Here is one California-style.

Cooking For One— A Challenge

The main obstacle for us "singletons" to overcome is to convince ourselves that we are really worth cooking for. We think of cooking something especially good to eat or prepare, then we change our minds saying "why cook this just for me?"

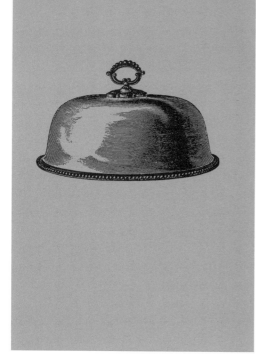

There are ways to overcome this; either decide that you are worth it or invite a friend to share it with you or, better yet, decide that it is a good meal to make just for the leftovers to store in the freezer for one of those days when you are too busy to cook. Do not be afraid to have leftovers. Freezers and microwaves have completely changed the cooking-for-one meals. Food reheated in the microwave does not have a leftover taste.

Actually, there are many advantages in singles cooking:

- You do not have to have certain foods cooked at any given time, so you cook when you are in the mood.

- You can experiment; you can try different combinations and flavors just for yourself. My friends come up with some very unusual combinations when doing this that just happen to be very delicious.

- You do not have to question if you should put green peppers in your meatloaf.

- It is so easy to prepare a complete meal for one in the microwave in about 15 minutes when you are in a hurry. Here are a few examples.

Cooked Cabbage and Apples

1/2 medium size head of cabbage, chopped
3 medium apples (if they are nice red ones do not peel, just core and chop)
1 t. salt

Combine in heavy saucepan with just enough water to keep from burning; bring to boil; simmer, watching closely until tender. They cook quickly. From here you can go your own way. I added 2 tablespoons of cider vinegar. My apples were quite mild so I needed the vinegar.

I served this in a side dish and did some experimenting with herbs. Dill was good, thyme gave it a sagey taste, parsley is a good addition and, of course, caraway seed is always good with cabbage. You might want to add a tiny bit of sugar, start with a teaspoon at a time. You can't go wrong; when it tastes good, eat it!

The other day I found apples and cabbage in the refrigerator. I decided to cook them together.

A friend inspired me to make some homemade vegetable soup recently. It had been years since I had made soup from a soup bone; I found that our markets still sell them. I used my pressure cooker for making the broth.

Vegetable Soup

1-1/2 lbs. soup bone and meat
1 small onion sliced   1 t. salt
Dash of pepper

You can cook this in a quart of water until meat falls off the bone or process in the pressure cooker at 15 pounds pressure for 50 minutes. Remove meat and bones and strain broth. I let this cool to remove fat. Return broth and meat only to cooker and add your favorite vegetables. I used:
4 carrots, finely chopped
1/2 of a small rutabaga, finely chopped
1 medium onion, finely chopped
2 potatoes, chopped

Simmer this soup over one hour and season to taste.

To make delicious soup, you can use the canned broth which is very good, omitting the first part of this recipe. This soup freezes well and tastes delicious reheated. I have put small containers of it in the freezer for future lunches.

Lamb Dinner For One

I bought 2 cubed lamb patties, put one in the freezer and grilled one for dinner. This takes just a few minutes. I baked a potato in the microwave and made a tossed salad. Mint or currant jelly adds a perfect touch to any lamb dish. Our markets now have a good variety of meats in small packages, especially good for us singles.

Sometimes I think that we all crave a real meat-and-potatoes meal like this next one, which can be prepared in about 20 minutes at the most and there are no leftovers.

*T*hen there is the time when we feel like making a lemon meringue pie; it's the time to invite helpers to eat it. Which brings us to the idea of entertaining.

We singles must invite someone to eat with us occasionally or we get into a rut. You can console yourself when this happens by telling yourself that "I do not have the time or space to entertain," or "I'll do it next year" for excuses. We soon learn, however, that friends are the bottom line for us and Emerson put it this way when it comes to etiquette. "Manners are the happy way of doing things." I like that. To make it easy for yourself, invite people you like for themselves, people with whom you have interests in common. It will not matter if the dishes do not match and the molded salad does not unmold. This way your friends will have fun because they are like each other.

Your friends will love this very special dessert and no baking required.

Coconut Cream Dessert Dip

1/3 C. coconut, shredded
1 C. marshmallow cream
2 to 3 T. red raspberry preserves
1 C. sour cream
1/4 C. walnuts, chopped (optional)
Mint leaves, if desired

Fruit for dipping (whole strawberries, green grapes, pieces of cantaloupe and watermelon, nectarine and apple slices)

Spread coconut in 9-inch glass pie plate. Microwave, uncovered on medium-high until light brown, 3 to 4 minutes; toss with fork after each minute. Cool.

Microwave marshmallow cream in medium bowl, uncovered on medium-high until softened, 1 minute. Stir in preserves until smooth. Stir in toasted coconut. Add sour cream and walnuts; mix well. Spoon into serving bowl; cover and refrigerate until chilled. Garnish with mint leaves. Serve with fresh fruit for dipping.

Company Meals

It seems that company meals are out of style. Now we go out to our favorite restaurant, making it easy on the cook; however, looking back, I like to recall the Sunday dinners when we were growing up. Sunday was when we had company or went to a relative's home for the best meal of the week. Restaurants were not available in the Thumb area of Michigan at that time, and we would never dream of going to one anyway.

Our fathers were dressed in their best Sunday suits and the women still were wearing their church dresses topped with frilly aprons. The tables were covered with a white tablecloth, and chicken was usually the main dish, along with mashed potatoes, gravy and biscuits. We were expected to use our best table manners.

I feel that, for our children's sake, we need company dinners. It is my opinion that young children should be taught good table manners at a very young age so it will be natural for them to handle any situation later in their lives. Table manners inspire tact, diplomacy and respect for others at the table or anywhere else; it is important to their future. We oldsters, who were taught to come to the table only when dinner was served, asked for food with "please" and "thank you" and "May I be excused?" when leaving the table, are appalled at the lack of good training on the part of the younger generation.

Enough from an old-fashioned grandmother. Let's plan a company dinner. I am reminded of a menu like the following that was quite popular awhile back. You don't need to stay home all day; your roast is cooking slowly in the oven and needs no attention; your salad could be made the night before, and what could be better than cookies and ice cream for the kids of all ages? Grandmother would have pickles, olives and jelly on the table, so let's not forget these colorful items for our beautiful table.

Our dinners are more casual now, often served cafeteria-style, where everyone fixes his own plate, and I am all for it. I love the fun of doing this. Yet even here good manners are so very necessary to show respect for our host or hostess who has prepared this meal. I love placemats, paper plates and napkins; yet, I know that we need to know how to use fine china, crystal and silver without mishaps or confusion.

MENU

Pot Roast with Rice
Tart Perfection Salad
Jiffy Beans and Pineapple
Hot Rolls or Biscuits
Ice Cream and Cookies or
Strawberry Shortcake

Pot Roast With Rice

1 4-1/2 lb. lean chuck roast
3 t. salt
1/4 t. pepper
1 C. uncooked rice

Brown meat on both sides in heavy skillet; season with 2 teaspoons salt and pepper. Line a 9 x 13-inch pan with heavy-duty aluminum foil, allowing foil to fold over to seal. Place meat in center of foil-lined pan; pour drippings over meat; seal ends and sides of foil tightly. Roast in 250-degree oven 2-1/2 to 3 hours. Open foil, being careful to save all meat liquid. Place rice in meat broth; season rice with 1 t. salt; seal foil again. Return to oven 1 hour longer until rice is tender. Makes 6 servings.

Tart Perfection Salad

1 pkg. lemon-flavored gelatin
1 C. boiling water
1 C. cold water
1 t. salt
2 T. lemon juice
1/2 C. finely diced celery
1 C. finely-shredded cabbage
1/3 C. chopped radishes
1/3 C. chopped green pepper
Lettuce
Mayonnaise

Dissolve gelatin in boiling water; add cold water, salt and lemon juice. Chill until partially set; fold in vegetables. Pour into 5-cup ring mold; chill until set. Unmold on lettuce leaves; serve with mayonnaise. Makes 6 servings.

This salad will complement the pot roast and rice.

Grandma always had a dish of baked beans on her Sunday dinner table. Here is an easy recipe; it has a beautiful crusty top and the flavor is delicious.

Our modern cooks also prepare entrees as main one-dish meals, combining the wonderful flavors of meat, vegetables, pasta and seafood. My granddaughter, Diana, recently gave me a couple of recipes for entrees she used to feed her two growing sons and one hungry husband.

Jiffy Beans and Pineapple

2 cans (1 lb. ea.) pork and beans
1 can (14 oz.) chunk pineapple, drained
2 T. brown sugar
1/4 t. ginger
2 t. soy sauce

Pour beans into greased baking dish or casserole; cover with well-drained pineapple. Sprinkle with brown sugar, ginger and soy sauce. Bake in 350-degree oven 25-30 minutes. Serves 8.

Special People and Places

Tomato and Basil Fettuccini

1/4 C. chopped onions
1 clove garlic, minced or finely chopped
1/4 C. olive oil
3-1/2 C. (28 oz. can) tomatoes
1 T. dry basil
1 t. salt
1/2 t. pepper
1 box (12 oz.) fettuccini

Cook the onions and garlic in oil, add the tomatoes and seasonings and simmer, uncovered, 15 to 20 minutes. Serve along with the fettuccini cooked according to directions on the box. If you want a meal-in-a-dish, cook a pound of hamburger with the garlic and oil.

Old-Fashioned and Modern Entrees

From my dictionary, I quote: "Entrees, the principal course at a meal. In lavish formal dinners a dish served between the fish and meat course or directly before the main course."

The old cookbooks have chapters on entrees with many recipes such as chicken force-meat, aspic jelly, chicken timbales or souffles and all kinds of fish timbales or mousses. They also have lots of croquettes.

I wonder as I read these old books, where they found the time to cook the way they did. They most likely had a hired girl or an older daughter trained to help in the kitchen. Boiled tongue, fried calf's liver and veal loaf were served, as well as calf's foot jelly. These old books also had a chapter on vegetable entrees alone.

Diana served this potato dish and I found it delicious, especially since I am a potato-lover from way back.

I have a couple of recipes that I think are ideal entrees. I cannot explain how things happen the way they do, but last week when I was hungry for old-time spoon bread and prepared half a recipe just for myself, the same day I received this next recipe; they are just plain delicious with lots of butter, bacon or sausage and honey or syrup.

Diana's Potato Casserole

1 pkg. frozen hash browns (2 lbs.) thawed enough to break up
Up to 8 oz. sour cream
1 can cream of chicken soup, undiluted
2 to 3 C. shredded Cheddar cheese (3 C. is better)
1 medium onion, diced
Salt and pepper to taste (Go easy here, as there is salt in the soup)

Grease 13 x 9-inch dish and preheat oven to 350. In a large bowl, mix all ingredients together and put in baking dish.

Topping:

(Optional, though it is beautiful and tasty)

2 C. corn flakes, crushed; 1/4 C. butter or margarine, melted. Mix and put on top of potatoes. Bake 45 minutes or until bubbly. Makes 12 servings.

Spoon Bread

1 qt. milk   1 C. yellow corn meal
1-1/2 t. salt   2 T. butter or margarine
4 eggs

In double boiler or at low heat, heat the milk. Stir in corn meal and salt; cook, stirring to a thick mush. Start oven at 400 degrees. Remove mush from heat and add butter. In bowl, beat eggs until well blended. Stir into mush. Pour into well-greased 1-1/2 qt. casserole. Bake, uncovered for 50 to 55 minutes. Serve at once with lots of butter as the bread for the meal. I find that this is also good reheated in the microwave as you need it.

So here are two delicious recipes for Spoon Bread:

*T*he second recipe came from Lillian Biggs of Hilton Head Island and is made more as a main dish with vegetables. I also made this spoon bread and had helpers to eat it—they approved.

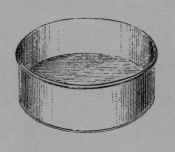

Harvest Vegetable Spoon Bread

Butter
Cornmeal
2 t. butter
1/2 C. chopped onion
1/2 C. cornmeal
1/2 t. salt
1 C. water
3/4 C. (3 oz.) shredded Cheddar cheese
4 eggs, separated
1 C. milk
2 t. prepared mustard
1 t. Worcestershire sauce
1/4 t. pepper
1-1/2 C. (10 oz.) frozen vegetables, thawed and drained (such as broccoli, cauliflower and carrots)
1/2 t. cream of tartar

Lightly butter bottom and sides of a 2-quart souffle dish or casserole. Dust with cornmeal. Set aside. In medium saucepan over medium heat, cook onion in butter until tender, about 4 or 5 minutes. Remove from heat. Stir in cornmeal and salt. Gradually stir in water until smooth. Cook and stir over medium heat until thickened, about 4 minutes. Stir in cheese until melted. Blend in egg yolks, milk, mustard, Worcestershire sauce and pepper until smooth. Stir in vegetables. Set aside.

In large mixing bowl, beat egg whites with cream of tartar at high speed until stiff but not dry. Gently fold reserved yolk mixture into whites using a rubber spatula. Carefully pour into prepared dish. Bake at 375 degrees until puffy and golden brown and mixture shakes slightly when oven rack is gently moved back and forth. This takes about 55 minutes.

Chocolate Pudding

3 T. cocoa
3 T. flour
6 T. sugar
1/4 t. salt
1 egg, well beaten
2 C. milk
1 t. vanilla

Mix cocoa, flour, sugar and salt together; add milk and egg. Cook over boiling water until thick; add vanilla. Cool and serve. Makes 6 servings.

Puddings

Puddings were one of the most popular desserts in great-grandmother's time. The old cookbooks had many pages for puddings, which had to be made from scratch. Our country was mainly populated by farmers, so there was always milk, bread or corn meal on hand to make a hasty pudding.

Now we can buy mixes to make all kinds of puddings and they are good. Some we do not even need to cook and others are already in small cups for the lunchbox. Most of these puddings are just as good as those we make. However, I like the old-time flavor of homemade puddings and other old stand-bys. I still make this one from my recipe file card, which is now yellow with age.

Grandma's bread did dry out and when a recipe called for bread crumbs they already were dry. She did not have an electric refrigerator or freezer to keep her bread moist, so she made bread pudding. This was the first bread pudding I ever made and I still think that it is one of the best.

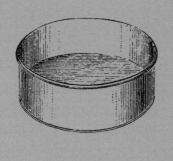

Bread Pudding Deluxe

2 C. milk, scalded
2 T. butter
1 C. bread, cubed
1/3 C. sugar
1/4 t. vanilla
1/2 T. almond extract
2 eggs, slightly beaten
1 C. shredded coconut

Combine milk, butter and bread cubes; add sugar, salt, and flavoring to eggs, beating slightly. Pour milk mixture over egg mixture; Add coconut. Pour into greased baking dish; put in pan of hot water. Bake in 350 degree oven 45 to 50 minutes. Makes 6 servings.

Rice Pudding

1/2 C. rice   1 t. salt
1/2 t. nutmeg   4 T. sugar
1/2 C. seeded raisins   4 C. hot milk
2 C. cold milk

    Mix first six ingredients together; pour into buttered pudding dish. Cook in 300-degree oven 2 hours, stirring occasionally the first hour. At the end of 2 hours add cold milk; cook 30 minutes longer. Serve with sugar and cream. I made this one time when I had lots of time and loved it.

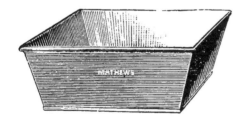

Rice pudding was another favorite of our grandmothers. Their timing was so different from the way we do it; they steamed puddings of all kinds in a steamer for hours; they could set them back on the wood range for half a day. Steamed puddings were very popular. She would not believe our wonderful ovens and microwaves.

Let me tell you about mother's waterless cooker. A coffee man used to come regularly to sell coffee, tea and other products. By saving tokens she earned a waterless cooker—it probably was a 6-quart aluminum kettle with a cover with clamps to hold it down. She could put a roast in the bottom (it did need some water here) and it had a top compartment, which was big enough to steam rice or rice pudding.

It always has been a question whether to put raisins in rice pudding or not. Some people definitely wanted them and others not. This next recipe must have been made by one who liked them.

Tomato Pudding

*T*hen last, but not least, is old-fashioned tomato pudding. I have given you this recipe before, but I am repeating it because I have had a number of people ask me for the recipe. This is modernized a little, using dry hamburger or hot-dog buns, which give it an old-fashioned texture and canned tomato puree—grandmother had to put stewed tomatoes through a sieve for this ever popular pudding.

Dried hot-dog or hamburger bun cubes, to fill an 8 x 8-inch pan 1-1/2 inches deep.
2 cans tomato puree
1/2 to 1 C. sugar to taste
1/8 t. salt

Mix puree, sugar and salt together; pour mixture over bread cubes. Bake in 375-degree oven 30 minutes.

This can be baked while other food is cooking in the oven. Grandmother often put her whole dinner in the oven at the same time. Remember "The proof of the pudding is in the eating." You won't have leftovers.

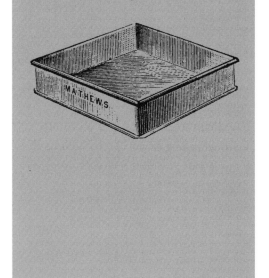

Weights and Measures

Standard Abbreviations

t.—teaspoon
d.b.—double boiler
T.—tablespoon
B.P.—baking powder
C.—cup
oz.—ounce
f.g.—few grains
lb.—pound
pt.—pint
pk.—peck
bu.—bushel
qt.—quart

Guide to Weights and Measures

1 teaspoon=60 drops
1 pound=16 ounces
3 teaspoons=1 tablespoon
1 cup=1/2 pint
2 tablespoons=1 fluid ounce
2 cups=1 pint
4 tablespoons=1/4 cup
4 cups=1 quart
5-1/3 tablespoons=1/3 cup
4 quarts=1 gallon
8 tablespoons=1/2 cup
8 quarts=1 peck
16 tablespoons=1 cup
4 pecks=1 bushel

Substitutions and Equivalents

2 tablespoons of fat=1 ounce

1 cup of fat=1/2 pound

1 pound of butter=2 cups

1 cup of hydrogenated fat plus 1/2 t. salt=1 cup butter

2 cups sugar=1 pound

2-1/2 cups packed brown sugar=1 pound

1-1/3 cups packed brown sugar=1 cup of granulated sugar

3-1/2 cups of powdered sugar=1 pound

4 cups sifted all purpose flour=1 pound

4-1/2 cups sifted cake flour=1 pound

1 ounce bitter chocolate=1 square

4 tablespoons cocoa plus 2 teaspoons butter=1 ounce of bitter chocolate

1 cup egg whites=8 to 10 whites

1 cup egg yolks=12 to 14 yolks

16 marshmallows=1/4 pound

1 tablespoon cornstarch=2 tablespoons flour for thickening

1 tablespoon vinegar or lemon juice & 1 cup milk=1 cup sour milk

10 graham crackers=1 cup fine crumbs

1 cup whipping cream=2 cups whipped

1 cup evaporated milk=3 cups whipped

1 lemon=3 to 4 tablespoons juice

1 orange=6 to 8 tablespoons juice

1 cup uncooked rice=3 to 4 cups cooked rice

Index

Special People and Places